THE COLLAPSE OF CONSTITUTIONAL REMEDIES

INALIENABLE RIGHTS SERIES

. . .

SERIES EDITOR
Geoffrey R. Stone

Geoffrey R. Stone
EDWARD H. LEVI DISTINGUISHED SERVICE
PROFESSOR
UNIVERSITY OF CHICAGO LAW SCHOOL

Laurence H. Tribe
CARL M. LOEB UNIVERSITY
PROFESSOR OF LAW
HARVARD LAW SCHOOL

David A. Strauss
GERALD RATNER DISTINGUISHED SERVICE
PROFESSOR OF LAW
UNIVERSITY OF CHICAGO LAW SCHOOL

Mark V. Tushnet
WILLIAM NELSON CROMWELL
PROFESSOR OF LAW
HARVARD LAW SCHOOL

Kathleen M. Sullivan
STANLEY MORRISON PROFESSOR OF LAW
STANFORD LAW SCHOOL

J. Harvie Wilkinson III
JUDGE
US COURT OF APPEALS FOR THE FOURTH
CIRCUIT

Cass R. Sunstein
ROBERT WALMSLEY UNIVERSITY PROFESSOR
HARVARD LAW SCHOOL

Kenji Yoshino
CHIEF JUSTICE EARL WARREN PROFESSOR OF
CONSTITUTIONAL LAW
NEW YORK UNIVERSITY SCHOOL OF LAW

GEOFFREY STONE AND OXFORD UNIVERSITY PRESS GRATEFULLY ACKNOWLEDGE THE
INTEREST AND SUPPORT OF THE FOLLOWING ORGANIZATIONS IN THE INALIENABLE
RIGHTS SERIES: THE ALA THE CHICAGO HUMANITIES FESTIVAL THE AMERICAN BAR
ASSOCIATION THE NATIONAL CONSTITUTION CENTER THE NATIONAL ARCHIVES

The Collapse
of Constitutional
Remedies

Aziz Z. Huq

OXFORD
UNIVERSITY PRESS

OXFORD
UNIVERSITY PRESS

Oxford University Press is a department of the University of Oxford. It furthers
the University's objective of excellence in research, scholarship, and education
by publishing worldwide. Oxford is a registered trade mark of Oxford University
Press in the UK and certain other countries.

Published in the United States of America by Oxford University Press
198 Madison Avenue, New York, NY 10016, United States of America.

© Oxford University Press 2021

CIP data is on file at the Library of Congress
ISBN 978–0–19–755681–8

DOI: 10.1093/oso/9780197556818.001.0001

1 3 5 7 9 8 6 4 2
Printed by Sheridan Books, Inc., United States of America

Contents

...

Acknowledgments

...

I am grateful to Andrew Coan, Seth Davis, Neal Devins, Gerald Magliocca, Tara Leigh Grove, Alon Harel, Jon Michaels, Jim Pfander, Aziz Rana, Shalev Roisman, and Gerry Rosenberg. All read parts of the manuscript and gave me valuable feedback. Geof Stone read a proposal and the whole draft. At both stages, he gave thoughtful and useful reactions. Genevieve Lakier and I wrote a piece together that spun out some ideas related to this book; in the process, we had many thought-provoking conversations. Deans Michael Schill and Tom Miles of the University of Chicago Law School nurtured a robust intellectual home for work on this volume. The *Duke Law Journal*, the *Northwestern University Law Review*, and the *University of Chicago Law Review* all published pieces that prefigure parts of this argument. None of this book's text is drawn directly from those pieces. I have substantially reworked my ideas since those writings, but the editors at those journals all did terrific work sharpening my arguments. University of Chicago Law students Becca Hansen and Simon David Jacobs proofed a draft of this book and made many fine suggestions. Finally, the Frank J. Cicero Fund provided financial support.

ACKNOWLEDGMENTS

Much of this book was written with my sons, Kian and Corin, in the house, during the cloistered summer of 2020. As wearisome and dull as it was for them to be home through the pandemic, it was a balm for me to have them close to hand as the world curdled and shrunk. Without them, and my wife, Margaret, there would be scant reason to argue for a better future.

Introduction

We're all federales.

Associate Justice Antonin Scalia[1]

IN THE SPRING of 2020, two litigants seeking a remedy for a constitutional wrong arrived at the US Supreme Court's bronze door. One succeeded; the other was turned away. The difference in outcomes embodies two trends: the current collapse of remedies against illegal state violence, and a rising use of the Constitution for regressive deregulation. The first litigant, Seila Law LLC, was a California law firm that hangs its shingle next door to the Orange County Assessor's Office. It offers advice to individuals on how to manage debts. Seila Law found itself in trouble when the federal Consumer Finance Protection Bureau (CFPB) fingered it for charging clients illegal fees for debt-related services, and then lying about those fees. Rather than fighting those allegations, or complying with a bureau request for documents, Seila challenged the CFPB's constitutionality in federal court.[2] It complained that the president did not have enough control over the bureau's director to satisfy Article II of the Constitution. The lower courts considered and rejected this argument, so Seila Law appealed to the US Supreme Court.

The second case started in 2014. At the time, Alexander Baxter had been living homeless and on the street in Nashville, Tennessee. One day, he was arrested by two police officers for trying to break into a home, allegedly trying to steal electronics. The officers cornered Baxter in a basement. He turned to face them and raised his hands high in the air. Rather than handcuffing or arresting him, the officers set a police dog on Baxter. The dog leaped and bit him, sending him to the hospital. Invoking a Civil War–era statute that allows individuals to sue officials for unconstitutional actions, Baxter filed a complaint asking for damages. The federal trial court and the Court of Appeals dismissed his case. They did so without even addressing the question of whether his constitutional rights had been violated. Rather, both applied a doctrine of "qualified immunity." This rule barred any hearing unless Baxter could show not only that the officers had violated the Constitution but also that they'd done so in an especially serious way.[3]

As 2020 began, Seila Law and Baxter both found themselves before the US Supreme Court. Both asserted facially plausible constitutional claims. Both, though, had lost in the lower courts. That's where the similarities ended. Seila Law had its case heard on the merits—and won. The Court directly moved to the question of constitutionality, ignoring the procedural obstacles of the case. The decision in *Seila Law v. CFPB* didn't turn on whether the constitutional violation at issue was egregious. It didn't ask if Seila Law had been harmed by the alleged constitutional flaw or investigate whether Seila Law would have been treated differently if the president had greater control over the bureau. Instead, the Court delivered a smarting rebuke to Congress. It then invalidated a section of the statute creating the CFPB, albeit not enough to hobble the bureau entirely.

Baxter, in contrast, didn't get past the courthouse door. His petition to have the lower court decision reconsidered, filed by skilled lawyers at the ACLU, was turned aside without explanation. The lower court's ruling was left undisturbed. In the end, Baxter lost without any federal judge even looking at the question whether his constitutional rights had been violated. The Supreme Court declined to hear his case despite a slew of commentary from critics and Justices, casting doubt on the wisdom of "qualified immunity" after the 2020 death of George Floyd in Minneapolis.

Why the difference? The gap between Seila Law's and Alexander Baxter's fates turned on the availability of a remedy for a constitutional wrong. The Constitution contains many legal rules and rights. None enforces itself. Without a remedy, a right has no practical value. Remedies depend in the last instance on judicial action. Courts, that is, do not and cannot merely interpret the Constitution. If their work is to have practical value, they must also assign remedies in the form of damages, injunctions, or declarations as a way of giving practical effect to constitutional rights and rules. Congress might give courts remedial power to act, but at the end of the day, it is the courts and the courts alone that decide whether or not to use that power.

This is a book about how and when we have remedies for constitutional wrongs—and, more importantly, when and why we don't. Remedies are not doled out in an even-handed way. On the one hand, individuals and firms like Seila Law that bridle against government regulation tend to have an easy glide path into federal court. Their complaints often—but not always—relate to structural limits on the power of government to regulate or act at all. Their arguments, that is, hinged on principles of separation of powers and federalism, which the Court has drawn from the Constitution's design, not its text. But when an individual challenges illegal violence physically inflicted by a particular government agent as a violation of constitutional rights, the Court takes a less hospitable view. Baxter's travails illustrate a larger swath of cases where federal courts now provide no effectual response to unlawful state violence. This is not for want of rights. The Constitution contains negative rights to protect individuals against demeaning or harmful treatment by government agents. These include the Due Process Clause, the Fourth Amendment's right against unreasonable searches and seizures, the Fifth and Sixth Amendments' protections against unfair criminal prosecution, and the Equal Protection Clause's rule against racially discriminatory action. The demand for remedies in relation to these rights is linked to socioeconomic and political marginalization. Alexander Baxter was typical in being vulnerable to state violence by dint of being impoverished and homeless. The courts' failure to remedy state violence against him, however, compounded that vulnerability. It left him physically harmed without redress, and it signaled to police that they could indulge freely in unlawful violence without consequences.

The present remedial vacuum for individual rights against coercion, coupled with the ascendance of structural constitutional litigation, means that judicial action on constitutional questions deepens economic, social, and racial hierarchies. This is not only a result of a recent rightward turn among federal judges (although it is that). More profoundly, it flows from the political economy created by the Framers' vision for judicial independence. It is bred in the constitutional bone.

This book tells the story of the rise and fall of constitutional remedies for unlawful state coercion. The collapse of remedies, mentioned in the title, has played out over the past fifty years. But it has a longer backstory that I aim to narrate. To explain today's remedial poverty, we need to understand why federal courts behave as they do. That historical inquiry, taking in the sweep of judicial history back to the Founding, is a first aim of this book. Along the way, we examine the idea that the federal judiciary is "independent" from elected leaders' larger political projects. Judicial independence as implemented by the US Constitution, it will turn out, can also be in tension with the moral aspirations commonly associated with the ideal of an independent judiciary.

THE REMEDIAL FUNCTION

Courts in the common-law tradition of the United Kingdom and the United States have long been viewed as the source of remedies for unlawful government violence. This practical judicial role, rooted in English law, long predates the distinctive American invention of "judicial review," which involves judges settling legal ambiguities in the Constitution.[4] Regardless of their disagreements as to abortion, healthcare, or legislative redistricting policy, almost all jurists concur that this ancient, remedial role of the courts is well warranted, even necessary, in theory. Without remedies, too many of us who have constitutional rights on paper would in fact find ourselves helpless at the sharp point of state power. A remedy from a court may not be the only way to mitigate state violence. But a regime without such remedies seems inconsistent with the rule of law.

What remedies might federal courts offer against unconstitutional state violence? Obviously, judges can hand out damages awards. They can also rule that evidence obtained in violation of the Constitution can't be used in a criminal trial. They can order the release of a defendant convicted in a trial that violated the Bill of Rights. More rarely, they can issue an order or injunction against future violence.

Across these remedial pathways, however, the Supreme Court has thrown up a series of hurdles in the last forty years. The most important of these derail relief for individuals' challenges to state violence unless a rights claimant can make an exceptional showing. She must demonstrate that the state actor acted not only unconstitutionally but also that their action was very obviously wrong. In other words, the Court has demanded a showing of personal "fault" before permitting a constitutional remedy. This hurdle applies across the spectrum of potential remedies. It also seeps into the very marrow of constitutional rights themselves.

In a suit for money damages, a series of "immunity" doctrines disallow private actors from even getting into court to challenge government action. Baxter's claim was derailed by qualified immunity. But that is only one among many immunities impeding relief. None, though, rest on clear statutory or constitutional text. All are the result of judges inferring constraints on individual remedies from the context in which the Constitution or relevant statutes were enacted. Few of these obstacles, in contrast, hinder litigants advancing structural constitutional arguments.

If the person who violated a constitutional right worked for the federal government, there is a second problem. Under a set of arcane rules recalling ancient rules of pleading, the Court has demanded that a plaintiff prove she has a right to proceed in court—called a "right of action"—as well as an allegation of constitutional harm. Having made this demand, the judiciary has recognized a right to sue federal officials for only a handful of constitutional rights, and even then proceeded to carve out many exceptions to suit. It has done so, we shall see, even though Congress has passed a statute setting out official liability that explicitly assumes the existence of a judicially created right of action for constitutional wrongs.

Matters aren't much better if you've been arrested, indicted, or prosecuted in a constitutionally flawed criminal justice process. It is possible to ask a court to set aside evidence obtained by unconstitutional police searches and interrogations. But in practice the Supreme Court has made these remedies scarce.

And for those cases that overcome these barriers, further obstacles await. The Court has developed a set of near-impenetrable barriers to foreclose individuals from developing an evidentiary record of many constitutional wrongs. This is especially relevant in discrimination cases. The best evidence of unconstitutional motive will often be in the defendant's files. Only where a racial category is written on a regulation's face will the courts squarely address the constitutional equality question. This stymies challenges by minority plaintiffs to discriminatory state coercion, while enabling claims by White plaintiffs against affirmative action in education and government contracting. Finally, from schools to prisons to police stations to the border, the Supreme Court has cultivated a thicket of "deference doctrines." These instruct judges to give the benefit of the doubt to state officials whenever they proffer a minimally plausible justification founded on public safety, national security, or foreign affairs concerns.

Today, in short, most individual constitutional wrongs that reach a federal court yield no remedy. And those cases are but a small subset of instances in which the Constitution is violated. An individual victim of a constitutional rights violation must have the stamina and resources to find a lawyer and pursue their cause. Most can't or won't, especially if they already face other challenges—say, economic or emotional—in their ordinary lives. The legal limits on constitutional remedies are yet further discouragement.

This status quo cannot be explained in simple ideological terms. Strikingly, these barriers have not all been the work of judges from one side of the partisan divide. There are, to be sure, pivotal opinions in which the Court has split along ideological grounds. But in other decisions, partisan alignments can't offer much by way of explanation. Nor do these judgments have a sound functional justification.

Of course, specific decisions are often defended in terms of their desirable consequences. But these defenses rest on hollow empirical premises. In their totality, the Court's limits on remedies also have an effect that is greater than the sum of its parts. Foreclosing a single remedy is one thing, but doing away with them all is quite another. Today, by and large, the state wields its hobnailed boot and billy club with no fear at all of reprisal or reproach.

Yet at the same time that access for individual claims based on unconstitutional state coercion has waned, it has become easier for regulated firms such as Seila Law to mount structural constitutional challenges to regulation. Invoking ideas of federalism or the separation of powers, a firm or (less often) an individual litigant can resist the application of federal regulatory regimes aimed at consumer protection, public health, biosecurity, or fraud prevention. As in Seila Law's case, the courts do not apply threshold constraints like immunities or the right-of-action doctrine. Sometimes, courts even skip over inquiry into whether an alleged constitutional violation would make any difference to how a regulated party would have been treated. Litigants in these structural challenges nevertheless gain an immunity to regulation. They delay or gum up a legal regime that would otherwise channel their behavior. The opportunity for state coercion, which might be used to enforce the regulation, never even arises.

The present system of constitutional remedies thus precludes victims of state coercion like Alexander Baxter from obtaining meaningful relief while enabling challenges to regulation such as Seila Law's. Its overall effect is regressive. In practice, that is, the system makes it easier for the state to avoid paying the costs of violent, unconstitutional coercion, often levied upon populations that are economically vulnerable and socially marginal in the first instance. At the same time, firms that already have a secure economic footing are often able to delay when regulation kicks in, or to derail new regulation. In so doing, they raise the cost of government interventions to fix market failures. This judicial subsidy for deregulation has plenty of takers. In contrast to individuals who find themselves subject to unexpected state violence, firms are already well positioned and well resourced to lobby for their preferred rules in both Congress and agencies. They have multiple chances to achieve their goals before a rule becomes law. And once that has happened, they have no shortage of lawyers when it comes to litigation.

REMEDIES AND THE DECENT STATE

The relationship between judicial remediation schemes and the project of a decent, humane state is complex and ambiguous. Even if courts perfectly enforced negative rights against state violation, this alone would check only *unlawful* state violence. It would not necessarily trim back the rapid twentieth-century growth of *lawful* state coercion. The judicial enforcement of negative rights also does nothing to arrest the growing economic and social inequalities (or absolute deprivations) that make people such as Alexander Baxter vulnerable to state violence in the first place. Lurking behind the collapse of constitutional remedies, therefore, is a longer and bleaker history of accumulating structural violence, the result of a fracturing labor market and a vanishing social safety net.

Courts are no panacea for this. A more fulsome remedial regime might legitimate a more onerous coercive state apparatus. Or it might cast light on the costs attendant on such a state—and hence sap public support for it. Or else it might enable more effective public protest and mobilization to challenge repressive and oppressive policies. It's hard to know in the abstract what would happen. Instead, a different, more subtle question may be worth pondering: What pathologies of state violence can courts "encase," and so insulate, from political pushback?[5] And which do they leave exposed to popular resistance?

A further irony is the predicament's democratic pedigree. America's federal courts are a product of both design and historical choices by the elected branches of the national government. Only by examining the original design and also its later democratic elaboration can we glean why and how the federal courts have come to fail the project of constitutional remediation for individuals. In this wider perspective, the relationship of courts to the wider national state becomes crucial. Anchored in constitutional clay, molded and contoured by the shifting demands of building a national state from the ground up, the federal courts are best understood today in terms of their relation to the larger political project of constructing national institutions for the American state. By situating the present remedial vacuum in a historical story of courts as the implements and outcome of a competition between different visions of American government, we better grasp the motives and effects of the federal courts.

THE BLUEPRINT FOR FEDERAL COURTS

The blueprint for the federal courts is to be found in the 1787 Constitution, and in particular its third Article. This blueprint was at once skeletal—a ghostly intimation of plural possible futures— and capacious. Indeed, it was only as later cohorts of presidents and legislators formulated their own understandings of the American state—driven by fleeting partisan and electoral incentives—and built upward from the Framers' inchoate design specifications, that the actual effects of federal courts on the polity would become clear. In the decades after the Constitution's ratification, what were once vague words on a parchment gesturing toward uncertain grandeur become first foundations and then a durable structure of load-bearing joists and beams. Courts became the institution familiar to us today only inch by inch via a gradual accretion of unexpected particulars.

What ensues today is misleadingly called "the Article III judiciary"—as if that scrap of text in the original Constitution somehow encompassed the institution that centuries of struggle over statebuilding would drag into being! That label erases the postratification path of contingent political choices taken by those who gave the courts resources, personnel, jurisdiction, and ultimately legitimacy. It misses the reasons why courts now can settle disputes without a sword or an army at their beck and call. It omits the winding road, replete with switchbacks and hairpin turns, that the courts have taken through larger political struggles over state power. Like many turns of originalist phrase, talk of an "Article III judiciary" is a tabula rasa upon which new ideological projects can be projected helter-skelter. Federal courts cannot be understood simply by looking at their blueprints any more than the architecture of a cathedral or skyscraper can be grasped by looking at a faded paper plan.

The contemporary poverty of individual judicial remedies for unlawful state coercion emerges from this volatile blend of an incomplete blueprint and a politicized dynamic of construction over time. It occurs because the judiciary is open by original design to pressure from partisan forces hostile or indifferent to some rights violation. It is a consequence of a long history of jurisdictional changes legislated by Congress, appointments by the president, and public campaigns by interest groups to influence or capture the judiciary. The doctrinal landscape of constitutional remedies is thus formed through the roving conflicts of national politics. Today, it is sharply inflected by a partisan formation, roughly aligned with the Republican Party, that disfavors constraints on the coercive state apparatus, dismisses concerns about racial discrimination against Blacks and other minorities, and opposes any effort to unleash the distributive potential of constitutional redress. A signal achievement of this partisan formation has been to fashion constraints on remedies that serve these ends, while leaving the courthouse door open to litigants such as Seila Law. All this under the emblem of an apparent fidelity to apolitical, historical "truth."

At the same time, partisan forces cannot completely explain the success of this antiremedial project. Several key decisions limiting actions for damages, motions for the exclusion of unconstitutionally gained evidence, and grants of release for state and federal prisoners garnered the support of bipartisan coalitions of Justices. To understand the strength of hostility to individual constitutional remedies means noticing that when the Constitution's drafters aimed, however falteringly, at an independent judiciary, they didn't pause to ask: independent to do what? They did not ask what an institutionalized judiciary, once it shrugged off the gravitational tug of partisan agendas (which, to be clear, it hasn't and can't always), would actually do. They did not anticipate how a powerful national judiciary (which emerged only at the end of the nineteenth century) would imagine its own interests. And they did not even consider the possibility that an independent judiciary's institutional interest would undermine, and not reinforce, constitutional rights.

But why should courts protect rights? The project of rights defense is labor intensive. It imperils the judiciary's prestige and position by putting it at cross purposes with the coercive state upon which it relies to enforce its orders. Remedies, in short, are at odds with the political economy that binds the federal judiciary into a larger national state. So regressive partisan formations disinclined to check coercive state power in its rawest form were pushing at an open door when it came seeking a penurious distribution of constitutional remedies for the Alexander Baxters of the world, while leaving the door open for its Seila Laws.

The federal courts are by institutional design inclined against the vindication of all constitutional rights against state coercion. They are, in contrast, primed to be solicitous of legal challenges to regulatory measures. The CFPB is one of these—an agency that protects ordinary borrowers and consumers from the sophisticated depredations of banks and payday lenders.

The link between politicians' ambitions for national state-building and judicial behavior, moreover, runs in both directions. Remedial redesign is a low-key way for courts to adjust the sorts of power the state can exercise. When the Court intervenes by modifying a remedy, its decision is rarely as newsworthy as when it announces a new right. Decisions about remedies are also technical. They are hard for nonspecialists to parse. Their practical effect often depends on how one particular remedy interacts with other remedial pathways, or the manner in which different parts of our legal system hang together. Thus, they cannot be understood in isolation. Rulings on habeas corpus review of criminal convictions, for example, have different effects depending on how state criminal courts are set up. Even jurists and experienced lawyers need to take a moment to think through their implications. What's more, whether a particular remedy matters or not often depends on whether ready substitutes exist.

Even if remedy decisions won't break any new ground in the culture wars, in short, they are an extremely important cog in the politics of judicial redistribution. They are one important way in which the federal courts shape public policy. It is how they decide whose ox is gored when government tackles the challenges of public safety, national security, or the creation and defense of markets.

WHAT JUDGES SAY

This story is at odds with judges' descriptions of their own roles and values. Indeed, what follows is an extended correction to common judicial rhetoric. In the most well-known opinion of the early nineteenth-century Supreme Court, Chief Justice John Marshall said that "[w]here a specific duty is assigned by law, and individual rights depend upon the performance of that duty, it seems equally clear that the individual who considers himself injured has a right to resort to the laws of his country for a remedy."[6] Speaking at Harvard Law School more than a century later, Chief Justice Charles Evans Hughes echoed the same thought. "Liberty in the long run cannot be secured," he said, without "recourse to independent and impartial tribunals where the announced common understandings which we call laws are enforced."[7] More recently, Chief Justice John Roberts has responded to criticism of the federal judiciary as a partisan body by insisting that the "independent judiciary" is "something we should all be thankful for."[8] A plumb line in this rhetoric is the notion that judicial independence has helped realize individual rights and the rule of law.

Talk of this kind is best viewed as compensatory, not descriptive. By design and historical development, federal courts are simply not well adapted to providing remedies for the violation of negative rights against state violence. For most of their history, the federal courts have indeed played a minor role in this enterprise. They have instead played a more important role in drawing bounds on what the regulatory state can do. We should not expect federal courts as presently organized to play any large role in a redistributive political agenda. A regressive impulse is too breed close to the institution's heart. Absent a firm direction from both elected branches, the historical tendency and institutional inclination of the federal judiciary will instead lean toward regressive support for the coercive state twinned with hostility toward redistributive regulatory initiatives.

To some, the best progressive reform of the courts might seem to be complete emasculation, not legitimating reform. But this may well go too far. Without a robust defense of negative rights against state coercion and contempt, marginalized groups face serious impediments to effective organizing and political action. To think that redistributive goals, or the political campaigns that they require, can be achieved by wholly disempowering the courts, therefore, is a mistake, even if courts won't be instruments of redistribution themselves. There's a good reason for movements such as Black Lives Matter to conjoin the goal of shackling police violence with a larger ambition of reviving the social state. The federal courts could play a positive role in the first project, as well as getting out of the way of the second through changes to their jurisdiction. Getting them to do so is imaginable as a political matter, even if it is unlikely to happen any time soon.

The ideals that the three Chief Justices invoked are often associated with a more general, regulatory ideal of the rule of law. So it might seem that skepticism of their claims implies a potentially destabilizing and corrosive view of the rule of law on my part. Not so. This last idea is an imprecise and contested concept, which can be cashed out in several quite different ways. Too often, "rule of law" talk is obfuscating rather than clarifying. Here, I use the term to capture the idea that those invested with state power remain subject to standing legal constraints, enabling citizens and residents to anticipate and plan their lives without fear of arbitrary state coercion. This is a minimal element of the rule of law, one that the Oxford legal philosopher Joseph Raz has termed a precondition rather than a constitutive element.[9] The rule of law goes wanting, that is, when state agents behave in unpredictable, and especially violent, corrupt, and predatory, ways. When settled expectations of bodily liberty and security are impossible to sustain, or when a person's race, religion, or the like works as a standing invitation to official contempt, ordinary people necessarily live with a background fear of the state that is at odds with the possibility of a minimally decent life—let alone the possibility of organizing to stake their claim in the democratic process.

With that conception in hand, the relation of judicial independence and the rule of law can be more clearly pinned down. We naturally think of courts as guardians of the rule of law.[10] But I insist here that, especially for the economically and socially marginal, the federal courts have not played this role (with fleeting exceptions) through American history. Today, the uneven supply of legality to litigants as different as Seila Law and Alexander Baxter suggests that the rule of law is a divisible good. It can be selectively supplied by courts to some while being denied to others. Worse, this can be achieved by courts in low-key legal disputes that quietly allocate the good of legality in unequal ways. To draw out this tension is emphatically not to doubt the value of the rule of law. Rather, it is to insist on that value by showing how current institutions fail to deliver it—and demanding that they henceforth do better.

The story of constitutional remedies that this book tells is a piece of the American legal tradition that does not get as much attention as it deserves. It has a marginal place in the law school curriculum. It also falls through the cracks of lawyers' conventional folk wisdom. By and large, the public account of the federal courts focuses relentlessly upon judges' articulation of rights and restrictions on state action without asking how the resulting rules then shake out on the ground. In particular, much ink is spilled on the power of courts to strike down statutes and declare the meaning of the Constitution—questions of "judicial review" and the problem of "counter-majoritianism." Important as these debates about judicial review are, they miss the gap that separates the abstract enunciation of the law on the books from its concrete implementation in practice. Legal scholars too often attend to questions of high theory but lose sight of the mundane work of making law stick on the ground. To be sure, the judicial powers to declare what the law is and to enforce the law on the ground often comingle and blur together. But they are conceptually and practically separate. My attention here is to the blue-collar labor of vindicating rights precisely at the seam at which state violence sparks brightly against human flesh.

Close engagement with the way in which constitutional remedies are doled out helps us think about the ways in which the courts fit within the historical development of state power in America. Liberal, conservative, progressive, or socialist—all ought to care about the way in which judicial action nudges or pulls the American state into coercive or meliorating shapes. For as much as it is a product of different partisan coalitions' efforts to shape the American state, the federal judiciary is a force that powerfully shapes the American state to our gain or to our cost, but not always in accord with our wills.

CHAPTER I

Blueprint

Eppur si muove.

Galileo[1]

IT IS THE start of the eighteenth century in the raw wilds of colonial America. A Pennsylvania woman is searching for a way to sell land to pay her husband's debts. Rather than going to a court, she turns to Pennsylvania's elected assembly. Its members debate. They then vote on the merits of the woman's claim as if they were judges. They rule against her.

This blend of the legislative and the judicial functions, so jarring to contemporary ears, was not unique to Pennsylvania among the colonies. In Massachusetts, citizens could file a petition for relief "by a Private Act, or by a Hearing" with their state assembly, and then secure legislative resolution of the matter. In several American colonies, assemblies behaved as courts, ruling on whether married couples could obtain divorces; whether individuals had committed treason; whether defendants should be issued with reprieves for their ordinary crimes; and even how previous legislative enactments should be interpreted. In the colonial world from which the American nation was born, courts did exist, but they had no monopoly on the ability to interpret and apply the law.[2] Instead, colonial judges commonly sat on legislative councils. Governors routinely heard appeals in civil cases. The King's Privy Council, sitting far away in London, heard appeals as well. The lines between what are now imagined as separate branches were pervasively blurred. Little wonder that future president John Adams would write in 1766 that "the first grand division of constitutional powers" lay between "those of the legislature and those of the executive." Little wonder he would opine before the Constitution's drafting that "the administration of justice" properly fell in "the executive part of the constitution."[3] Little wonder too he saw no role for courts independent of both the legislature and the executive.

Adams here was echoing the finest political scientists of the day. That science crystallized authoritatively in John Locke's 1690 *Two Treatises of Government*. Locke was no stranger to the heavy inequity of a repressive central state. In 1683, he had fled for refuge in Holland after being suspected of involvement in the Rye House plot to assassinate Charles II of Great Britain. He returned only in 1688 along with William and Mary of Orange to witness the Glorious Revolution, probably having written his famous treatises while in exile. In his second treatise, Locke offered an influential account of the separation of governmental powers. To American ears a century later, the Lockean ideal of separation was often taken as a useful means of disabling the dangerous excesses of a newly empowered national government.

Yet in Locke's telling, there was no separate judicial power. Just as in the English Constitution of the late 1600s, Locke's plan of government assimilated the courts into the executive. (Indeed, the highest court in England sat in the House of Lords—where it would remain until the twentieth century.) For Locke, a want of independent courts was no troubling matter. The needful separation of powers, in Locke's view, had to be carved between the executive and legislative branches.[4] "Independent" courts were nowhere in view in the institutional landscape.

Nor was this gap in the intellectual landscape filled by other sources. The other influential theorist of government design at the time of the Founding was the French aristocrat and man of letters Charles-Louis de Secondat, Baron de La Brède et de Montesquieu. Based on his rather rose-colored—and somewhat factually challenged—understanding of the ancient and unwritten "constitution" of English law, Montesquieu did talk about courts. But he saw them as "next to nothing." To the extent that he saw their promise, his argument hinged largely on the role of juries as "the judges of the nation," and not judges as such. Juries, he suggested, would act as frictions on errant state power.[5] Yet Montesquieu, like Locke, provided no template for a judiciary imagined as an autonomous institution with substantial power.

Historical practice provided no surer footing. The British metropole and her former colonies, to be sure, provided some examples of courts that stood apart from both legislative and executive branches—in particular, the King's Bench of the early seventeenth century. But the late-eighteenth-century landscape provided no good examples of how a constitutional designer could ensure judicial independence in practice. After the Declaration of Independence, early state constitution–makers thought of judicial independence as a problem of excessive executive branch control. Their view of courts was colored by their experience with the British Crown. As a result, these early constitution-makers strived to make courts more dependent on legislators. To this end, they installed judicial term limits, salary controls, and a legislative power to remove judges from the bench. As Thomas Jefferson commented, they largely succeeded at rendering the courts "a mere machine" at the state legislature's beck and call.[6]

But state legislatures later fell into popular disfavor because of their incompetence and inconsistency. Assemblies were alternatively hated for being too radical or else too much under the wealthy's thumb. As the 1780s wore on, a growing number of states also turned against plenary legislative control of the courts. By 1790, some nine out of thirteen had adopted some kind of tenure protection for judges during "good behavior." This shift turned out to be fleeting. A majority of state judiciaries were moved back to arrangements for picking judges via elections for fixed terms by the early nineteenth century.[7] The Republic would hence be characterized by a thoroughgoing "mingling of legislative and judicial functions . . . in important state jurisdictions" well into the nineteenth century.[8]

Nor was there a national model of an independent court. During the Revolutionary War, the states had lashed themselves together loosely through the Articles of Confederation. This first American constitution had not created a judiciary. Instead, the Continental Congress exercised all national power under the Articles and largely left the task of adjudication to the preexisting state-level courts.[9] Starting in 1780, that national assembly did take some steps toward forming a judicial body to hear appeals from state court decisions in maritime cases to decide who should have possession of goods and vessels seized on the high seas. But to the extent that this tribunal even got off the ground, it did not operate as a central national tribunal akin to today's Supreme Court.[10] Effectual judicial power instead remained dispersed among the several states.

So there was no colonial, state, or imperial model of an independent court that could be quickly transposed to the quite different scale of the new nation-state. To entertain the thought of independent federal judges in Philadelphia circa 1787, and to conjure up the means to embed that idea into the practical operation of a new government, was to embark on a wholly new and unguided enterprise.

In this intellectual and political context, the national judiciary that emerged from debates in Philadelphia's Independence Hall in 1787 was without real precedent. It was larger in scale and geographic reach than any precursor. It embodied a new and distinct theory of judicial independence. There was, to be sure, some precedent in state practice, but much also that was new and untried. And it achieved its independence though a blend of old and novel constitutional mechanisms. Fashioning these, the Constitution's drafters felt their way in darkness. They could not have known or anticipated how one choice about judicial power might rub and spark erratically when placed in tension with other, quite disparate moving parts in their constitutional creation. However much grew above them, these choices, whether spelled out in the text of Article III or implicit in its structure, remain today the vital foundations of the federal courts.

How then did Article III of the Constitution give flesh and form to the inchoate idea of judicial independence? The design of judicial independence flows though specific choices embodied in the Constitution's text, and we will examine those more intimately in a moment. But along with these textually manifest design choices, there is also a less visible substrate: a set of assumptions about the relationship of the courts to the political branches, and the behavior of federal judges themselves. These assumptions are largely spelled out in the nationalist politician Alexander Hamilton's scintillating essays in Federalist 78 and 79. There, the erstwhile West Indian offers a theory of judicial independence to fill the gap left by Locke and Montesquieu. Supple as a tendon, his theory knits the bare textual bone of Article III into a working model of judicial independence.

We shall see that Hamilton's logics turned out to be flawed.[11] But they foundered not because of any internal inconsistency. They failed rather because of events that occurred after he wrote, events that sapped his assumptions of empirical plausibility. Hamilton could not have predicted them. It is, though, an irony of sorts that Hamilton, like his friend and erstwhile collaborator James Madison, ended up playing a significant role in the later historical events that compromised his and Madison's constitutional design. Once its logic failed, the ideal of independence wrought in the textual blueprint in Article III of the Constitution became more fragile and porous still. In operation, it could not carry the weight of institutional independence. What emerged was not quite an independent judiciary—at least not immediately, and certainly not in the way that the generation of '87 might have anticipated.

THE CONSTITUTION'S BLUEPRINT FOR INDEPENDENT COURTS

The first three Articles of the 1787 Constitution describe three branches of government. They speak in turn of a Congress, an executive branch headed by a president, and a judiciary. But the parallelism stops there. Whereas Article I describes the new Congress in considerable detail, Article III offers only a bare sketch of the judicial branch. Looking back in time past the robust and extensive judicial institutions with which we are familiar today, therefore, reveals a relatively barren constitutional terrain. The text allows for the possibility of powerful courts, which might serve as guardians of individual rights. But it hardly guarantees such an outcome. In some ways, indeed, the constitutional terrain was quite unpropitious for the emergence of any sort of judicial independence.

To see why, observe first that judicial authority might be fashioned either by endowing the courts with institutional power or endowing individuals with judicial power. The Constitution does little on the first, institutional front. Its protection of independence, instead, hinges on the insulation of individual judges from improper influences.[12] This is a fragile and tenuous way of creating an independent court system.

In establishing a court system as an independent institution, two questions are central. First, what courts will there be? And second, what sort of matters can they hear? On both these points, the Constitution is equivocal. Its text directs the creation of only a Supreme Court and no "lower" federal courts. It allows, but does not require, Congress to create a set of lower federal courts "from time to time," as legislators see fit. A parallel provision in Article I seems to allocate to Congress the broad discretion to structure not only its own affairs but also those of the executive and the judiciary. As a result, there is a plausible argument (albeit a controversial one) that the text of Article III might be satisfied by Congress's creation of only one high court composed of one Chief Justice—with no associate justices and no lower federal courts.

Today, this seems well-nigh impossible. But from the perspective of 1787, and a baseline of no federal courts whatsoever, the prospect was far less outlandish. It would have left adjudication of federal law disputes to courts created by the existing several states, perhaps with occasional oversight supplied by the Supreme Court. This would have maintained, by and large, the status quo ante of 1787. Indeed, to suggest some other institutional arrangement was to invite resistance from those who benefited from state courts' dominant role.

Once a lower federal court has been created by Congress, moreover, the Constitution is silent as to whether there is any constitutional obligation to maintain that body. The document's text does not foreclose the possibility that legislators displeased with the behavior of a particular bench would simply dissolve it. And nothing in the Constitution speaks to the question of how federal courts enforce their orders against recalcitrant parties—especially ones with the backing of political heavyweights. Powerful actors might have cause to heed courts because they anticipate benefits from maintaining a general regime of compliance with court orders. If they anticipate elections in which power is transferred, perhaps they have some reason to husband judicial independence for self-protection at times when they are in opposition. But when pinched sharply by a particular decision, what stops them from defecting and ignoring the judges? The constitutional text provides no good answer.

The absence of a constitutional mandate to create lower federal courts was not foreordained. When James Madison arrived at the Philadelphia Convention in the spring of 1787, he had already drawn up a proposal for the new constitution's design. This was called the Virginia Plan. It anticipated a system of lower federal courts operating under a supreme court's aegis.[13] Some elements of this plan, such as a Council of Revision to supervise the constitutionality of state law, were decisively rejected in the Convention, much to Madison's dismay. In the heat of debate in Independence Hall, though, opposition also flickered into life against the idea of lower federal courts. Predictably, it blazed first from those concerned with protecting the authority and prestige of their own states' judiciaries. After Madison's Virginia colleague Edmund Randolph moved to embed a multitier national judiciary within the new constitution, another delegate, John Rutledge of South Carolina, objected that "State Tribunals might and ought to be left in all cases to decide in the first instance, the right of appeal to the supreme national tribunal being sufficient to secure the national rights & uniformity of Judgmts [sic]."[14]

Others complained of the great and needless expense of a new federal court system.[15] With the wind in his sails, Rutledge then successfully moved to strike the lower federal courts. It was only then that Madison and James Wilson stepped in with a compromise: Allow Congress to fashion lower federal courts, but don't do so directly in the Constitution. Their proposal, unfairly called the Madisonian (not the Madison-Wilson) compromise, ultimately carried the day by a vote of eight state delegations to two.[16]

Another keystone of courts' institutional authority is the idea of "jurisdiction." This opaque word simply means the kinds of disputes and cases that a tribunal is authorized to hear. A court without jurisdiction, at least in the Anglo-American tradition, is a court that is powerless to act. Drawing on this background well of legal concepts, the text of the Constitution provides a fairly detailed account of the kinds of federal-court jurisdiction that are possible. But once again, it leaves largely in congressional hands the choice of which kinds of jurisdiction will in fact be made available. Both the existence and the adjudicative authority of the federal courts, therefore, turn on legislative choice.

To be a touch more specific here, the text of the Constitution contained two lists. One describes the kinds of cases that the Supreme Court can hear. The other lists cases that the federal judiciary as a whole can entertain. The Supreme Court, for example, was endowed with jurisdiction to hear complaints involving "Ambassadors, other public Ministers and Consuls, and those in which a State shall be Party." Later, the Supreme Court would go on to rule that these were the only kinds of cases that could be filed directly in that body. For any other sort of dispute, the Supreme Court would have power to intervene only if there was an appeal from some other tribunal's ruling—and even then, it could act only if permitted to do so by Congress. On the other hand, the text of Article III describes a much wider range of disputes that Congress could—if it chose to—endow some "lower" federal court below the Supreme Court with the power to hear. Nine kinds of jurisdiction are listed, ranging from maritime disputes to cases in which a foreigner is suing one of the several states. Notice here an oddity of the Constitution's design: The jurisdictional reach of these potential inferior federal courts is much more capacious than the notionally superior Supreme Court.

Yet as there was no constitutional mandate for lower federal courts, there was no mandate to invest lower federal courts with any particular kind of jurisdiction. It was up to Congress to decide what cases they would hear. For example, the list of nine kinds of jurisdiction includes one called "federal-question jurisdiction." This includes disputes in which there was a question of law "arising under this Constitution, the Laws of the United States, and Treaties." A litigant like Seila Law or Alexander Baxter who had a complaint about the violation of a federal right could invoke this kind of jurisdiction. To a modern eye, this federal-question jurisdiction seems obviously central to what federal courts should be doing. Yet Congress did not get around to durably endowing federal courts with this species of jurisdiction until 1875.[17] Such jurisdiction flickered in and out of existence for a fleeting moment in 1801. But this interlude has had little enduring effect.

For almost all of the first century of the Constitution's existence, no federal court could hear a case simply because it involved a federal constitutional or statutory right. Instead, the great mass of business before the lower federal courts of the antebellum Republic relied on another form of jurisdiction called "diversity jurisdiction." That is, Article III allowed that the federal courts could hear "controversies . . . between Citizens of different states," without regard to whether those cases involved federal law or purely state law questions. The motivating assumptions behind diversity jurisdiction are disputed. But it seems likely that national legislators feared that state tribunals might be biased against out-of-state litigants, and so provided for an independent forum. In contrast, the Constitution's drafters may have thought that a federal court would be fair to all parties. This would matter, say, in cases where an out-of-state creditor sought to recover assets from an in-state debtor.[18] Whatever the ultimate justification for its creation, diversity jurisdiction turned out to be Congress's early workhorse when it came to fashioning lower federal courts through much of the eighteenth century.

Stripped to its essentials, the institutional judiciary envisaged by the Constitution was thus at first a skeletal affair. It needed legislative action to put flesh on its brittle bones. Jealous of potential competition to state courts, the Constitutional Convention abandoned the project of a compulsory national judiciary. Prioritizing the tensions of federalism, the drafters made an implicit concession cashed out in terms of the horizontal relations between branches of the federal government. Rather than creating co-equal branches, that is, Congress would have broad power to decide when and how federal courts could play a role in the new Republic. An apparent federal-state tension thus won out over worries about the need for a third branch as a counterweight to the national executive and legislature. Once a set of national courts had been created, moreover, there would be no essential or necessary core jurisdiction to a federal court. What effectual power that body could wield turned entirely on the caprice of elected national actors.

Such an outcome was far from inevitable. Surveying the national constitutions in operation today, it is possible to identify a range of measures through which an institutional judiciary can be infused with autonomy, and hence independence. A constitutional designer, for example, might incorporate a formal declaratory statement of judicial independence in constitutional text. Elsewhere, the Constitution does something like this for federalism in the Tenth Amendment: This provision affirms the persistence of some residual state sovereignty as well as the existence of unlisted individual rights. Alternatively, a constitution might create a compulsory grant of jurisdiction, vest a court system with control of its own budget, and otherwise restrain legislators' ability to eviscerate jurisdiction once it has been created. To be sure, none of these measures on their own guarantee the institutional robustness of a court system. But they would have provided a much surer foundation for judicial independence at an institutional level than the thin reeds woven into the 1787 text.

The Constitution, in sum, contains no meaningful protection for the institutional judiciary. It anticipates, to the contrary, the real possibility of a federal government largely operating without a judicial armature, much in the fashion of the Continental Congress and postcolonial state legislatures. Indeed, Congress would go on to create federal courts that handled only diversity cases, and not matters of federal law as such. Neither the drafters of the Constitution in Philadelphia nor those who participated in the ratifying debates aired any worry that the elected branches' control over jurisdiction would compromise or undermine the independence of the federal courts. There was also no extended discussion of the risk that political control of the institutional architecture of the judiciary might be in tension with some ideal of judicial independence.

INDEPENDENT JUDGES

If the institutional judiciary is weak, what then of the individual judge? There is something a touch quixotic about shielding an individual judge while the institutional judiciary remains so fragile a construction. What good can a single judge or justice do if she lacks the shield of institutional authority? Despite this puzzle, the Constitution pursues an exclusive strategy of individual insulation in the absence of institutional protection. The important question is how this is supposed to work.

Individual judges can be sheltered from external influences, whether from the elected branches or from an aroused public, in different ways. One approach would be to employ a nonpartisan selection process. Today, some thirty states use a form of merit selection for their courts. This frequently involves the use of a commission, which selects a panel of judicial nominees. From this panel, the governor selects a nominee. Such a selection process is coupled at times with back-end elections to determine whether a judge stays on the bench. These arguably extend a shadow back in time to shape judges' behavior in a fashion inconsistent with the ideal of independence.[19]

Alternatively, a constitution can use some kind of after-the-fact structure to shield judges from extrinsic efforts to meddle in particular cases. Such "ex post" mechanisms, as they are known, protect against a different risk from upfront, or "ex ante," safeguards. The latter is a way to prevent distortions in the selection of judges. The former assume selection to have worked out well, concentrating instead on the risk that improper influence may be brought to bear in a particular ongoing case or class of cases. They are, in other words, complementary rather than mutually exclusive ways of seeding judicial autonomy.

The Constitution opts for ex post devices for creating an independent judiciary, not ex ante ones. That is, its design focuses after the moment of appointment and not before. Once confirmed by the Senate and appointed, federal judges have a guaranteed salary that cannot be reduced during their time in office. Article III provides that a judge is to receive "at stated Times . . . for their Services, a Compensation, which shall not be diminished during their Continuance in Office." This rules out the possibility of fee-based compensation of the sort used in many colonial tribunals.

Such compensation systems gave judges a stake in how cases were resolved, and so raised red flags for early constitutional designers.[20] The Constitution does not address the risk that inflation will corrode the value of a judge's salary. That risk was hardly remote in 1787, since the Revolutionary period had witnessed serious price hikes. Indeed, it is startling to observe that Madison had initially proposed to the Convention that judicial salaries be fixed absolutely. This surprisingly myopic position was, wisely, rejected.[21]

Beyond a guaranteed salary, a federal judge is assured tenure of "office" so long as he or she manifests "good behavior." The Constitution, though, does not define "office." It hence leaves open the possibility that Congress might eliminate most, or all, of the jurisdiction exercised by a judge. It also seems possible, if less clear, that a judge could be moved from one federal court to another at Congress's discretion without being deprived of an Article III "office." That is, the text leaves open the possibility that the "office" in question is the station of Article III judge, or alternatively a position of judge on a specific tribunal.

However that question was resolved, Hamilton explained in the Federalist Papers that Article III's combination of salary and tenure protection would act as an "excellent barrier to the encroachments and oppressions of the representative body"—in other words, Congress. It would lead, predicted Hamilton, to "a steady, upright, and impartial administration of the laws." To craft the judiciary otherwise would be foolish, he warned, because "a power over a man's subsistence amounts to power over his will." What of age's ravages to the intellect of a life-tenured bench? Hamilton dismissed out of hand "the imaginary danger of a superannuated bench," given how "few there are who outlive the season of intellectual vigor."[22]

Hamilton's opponents in the ratification debates that raged between 1787 and 1789—now known collectively as the Anti-Federalists—agreed with his account of Article III in its broad strokes. But they drew a starkly different lesson. An important Anti-Federalist line of attack against the proposed constitution trained upon the wide discretion it allegedly afforded federal judges. The bench was, from the Anti-Federalists' vantage point, a touch too independent for the country's good. In January 1788, in the course of public debates over the Constitution's ratification, an Anti-Federalist going under the pseudonym "Brutus" described the federal courts as "altogether unprecedented in a free country. They are to be rendered totally independent, both of the people and the legislature, both with respect to their offices and their salaries. No errors they may commit can be corrected by any power above them."[23] This was not, Brutus clarified, a good thing.

Another Anti-Federalist, working under the nom-de-plume "Federal Farmer," concurred. The soi-disant agrarian warned that Hamilton and his peers were "more in danger of sowing the seeds of arbitrary government in this department [i.e., the judiciary] than in any other."[24] Yet another opponent of the Constitution, hailing from Georgia, echoed John Rutledge when he worried about the prospect of "strange and new courts" created by the Constitution working as a means "whereby our own [state] courts will soon be annihilated."[25] It was precisely the autonomy of the federal courts that concerned these writers. In contrast to colonial and early state arrangements, they worried, the new Constitution shifted power away from those most directly connected to the people, and into the hands of elite officials with only a tenuous connection to the public at large. Their alarm about the absence of popular control in national government would not have made much sense unless the Constitution's opponents, as much as its friends, believed that the judiciary had indeed been rendered autonomous of the elected branches of the government.

But this common ground among the proponents and opponents of the Constitution turned out to rest on fragile empirical ground. Contrary to the predictions of Hamilton, Madison, Brutus, and the Federal Farmer, the federal courts were not successfully disentangled at birth from popular and partisan politics. Instead, federal courts were to prove thoroughly porous to electorally related incentives. To understand why, however, it is necessary to turn from the Constitution's text to the assumptions that lay beneath its design choices—assumptions that are most crisply set forth by Alexander Hamilton.

THE WORKING ASSUMPTIONS OF JUDICIAL INDEPENDENCE

The assumptions animating Article III's design are not laid out in the Constitution's text itself. Rather, they infuse contemporary sources and commentary. These include records of the debate at Philadelphia in 1787 and the ratification debates in which pamphlets and newspaper articles flew back and forth as each of the thirteen then-existing states voted on whether to ratify the Constitution. The Philadelphia Convention's records are not terribly illuminating as to Article III. Indeed, "surprisingly little on the subject" of judicial independence was said during its debates.[26] When it did come to debating judicial selection, the main point of controversy seems to have been whether judges would be appointed by the president alone, or alternatively with the advice and consent of the Senate. Small states' representatives, jealous to defend their distinctive minority powers in the Senate, swayed the body in favor of the latter.[27] The jurisdictional provisions of Article III, meanwhile, were drafted by a Committee of Detail. They otherwise appear also to have provoked relatively little dispute.

In contrast to the thin gruel of the Philadelphia Convention, the ratification debates provide a richer source for understanding our judicial independence. In particular, there is a series of eighty-five essays written by Alexander Hamilton, John Jay, and James Madison., These were published between October 1787 and May 1788 under the pen name "Publius," in various New York newspapers, including the *New York Packet* and the *Independent Journal.* Scholars debate how important or influential these essays actually were.[28] The critical state of Virginia had ratified the Constitution on June 27, 1787, so its decision can hardly have been influenced by Publius's rhetoric or arguments. Whether the essays were influential in a specific state or not, Publius's arguments matter now because they are among the best available accounts of the underlying justifications for many of the critical elements of the constitutional design, written by men who were present during the Constitutional Convention and hence arguably better positioned than their contemporaries to surface the unspoken premises of the constitutional project.

A series of Alexander Hamilton's writings on the judiciary as Publius is a particularly rich source for understanding the presuppositions of the Founders' belief in an independent judiciary, and their confidence that the Constitution had in fact succeeded in creating one. From those writings can be drawn two separate baseline assumptions about how the new federal judiciary would operate. Seeing how and why these presuppositions falter is a first step to illuminating the current failure of the federal courts to supply remedies for the violations of individual rights, such as Alexander Baxter's Fourth Amendment interests.

A first presupposition of the Framers' conception of judicial independence concerned the composition of the judiciary, and, in particular, the personal character of the judges who would populate the federal bench. It was originally believed that the judiciary would be an effective bastion of the rule of law because of the way it was staffed. This belief arose because of—not despite—the involvement of political bodies (the Senate and the presidency) in judicial selection.

Hamilton offered two reasons for anticipating that only persons of integrity, free from disabling bias, would be appointed to the federal judiciary. The first appealed to the Senate's screening function. This scrim would in operation ensure the selection of persons of "intrinsic merit" and operate as an "excellent check" on presidential "favoritism" and "unfit characters."[29] Although not fully worked out, Hamilton's thought here seems to be that the Senate would operate as a constraining force on presidential choice of nominations. Knowing in advance that unqualified candidates will be rejected, a president would put forward only qualified ("fit") candidates for the federal judiciary. The argument that Hamilton made here might have been buttressed by a point that Publius (in fact, James Madison) made in an earlier Federalist paper. There Madison had argued that "successive filtrations" of candidates for national political office would ensure that only public-minded and virtuous officials would obtain power on the national stage.[30] Hence, state legislators would choose senators capable of exercising wisdom and discernment. With a virtuous Senate as sentinel, Publius thus suggests, even an occasionally errant president would be dissuaded from constitutional infidelity.

Notice, though, that Hamilton's argument applies not just to judges. It logically reaches all appointments within the executive branch subject to senatorial advice and consent. Yet Hamilton seems to suggest that judges will be made of different stuff from ambassadors, cabinet heads, or any other official subject to the Constitution's advice-and-consent mechanism. But his argument from Senate filtration offers no reason why this should be so. If judges are no different in temper or kind from other political appointees, the psychological justification for a durable form of judicial independence dims and falters.

In contrast, the second ground that Hamilton supplies for thinking that judges will have "intrinsic merit" does separate judges from other officials selected through presidential nomination and Senate confirmation. In Federalist 78, he developed a sociological argument from scarcity for the quality of the federal bench to directly quiet Anti-Federalist unease. "There can be but few men in the society who will have sufficient skill in the laws to qualify them for the station of judges," Hamilton predicted, and fewer still who "unite the requisite integrity with the requisite knowledge." Scarcity of legal talent, that is, would mitigate the risk of opportunistic or pernicious selection at either the presidential or Senate stages. Because it would not be feasible for the president to credibly nominate people lacking the requisite integrity for the federal bench, there would be simply no room for the White House to inject its own policy preferences into the appointment process.[31] The constitutional order relied not just on the forms of state action therefore, but upon the outputs of social action in the (legal) labor market.

Having developed this argument, Hamilton offered a second separate and distinct presupposition for the Framers' choices as to judicial independence—one that responded to the risk that judges might be inappropriately swayed in specific, individual cases. This argument also responded directly to the Anti-Federalist Brutus's concern that judges would be vested with a dangerous and "arbitrary discretion." To the contrary, insisted Hamilton. The nature of American law was such that federal judges would be "bound down by strict rules and precedent which serves to define and point out their duty in every particular case." The law, that is, was to be a technical and tightly integrated system. Of course, ambiguities and vagueness would sometimes trip up judges. But still, Hamilton insisted, judges would feel keenly the "duty" of legal compliance, and in particular the "inflexible and uniform adherence to the Constitution" that is expected of them.[32]

Hamilton's implicit model of the causal relationship between the law's rules and precedents on the one hand and the narrow scope of judicial discretion on the other would have seemed eminently reasonable during the Founding period. The period was characterized by a widespread belief that "judicial interpretation [was] constrained in a way that political decision-making was not," because the law was characterized by only "moderate indeterminacy." The Framers' account of an independent judiciary rested on this view of "law as sufficiently determinate and legislators sufficiently prescient for statutes to be self-applying."[33] This belief was not implausible at the time. There was a "relative paucity" of legislation in the early Republic.[34] With fewer statutes being produced, Congress might have enough time to examine carefully each of their verbal formulations and iron out ambiguities. Judges in the early Republic would thus be less likely to face unclear legal texts, conflicts between various statutes, or tensions between statutes and executive-branch regulations. Hence, the idea that law was characterized by only limited indeterminacy fitted well the observed corpus of law and widely shared expectations about legislative behavior in the early Republic.

HOW THE ASSUMPTIONS FAIL

Hamilton's assumptions supplied foundations for an individual (not institutional) and ex post (not ex ante) protection of judicial independence. But his assumptions did not survive the social and political transformations of the Republic's first decade. They were quickly eroded through processes for which, at least in part, Hamilton was himself responsible. The net result of this collision between constitutional theory and hard political realities was a shock: The federal courts were to prove not just institutionally dependent upon the caprices of the political branches, but also potentially vulnerable to ex ante political influence at the level of the individual judge. Of the mechanisms supporting judicial independence in Article III and beyond those Hamilton had flagged—the balancing and offsetting role of the Senate in relation to the presidency, the professionalism of the bar, and the disciplining effect of legislative drafting and judicial craft upon the bench's discretion—not one survived the 1790s. None withstood, that is, the social and institutional forces successfully unleashed by the new constitutional order.

Consider first the idea that the Senate would counteract the potential biases of presidential appointment. Hamilton assumes that the Senate would have distinct and adverse interests to the presidency. He relied implicitly on a theory of the separation of powers developed by Madison elsewhere in the Federalist Papers. According to this theory, "Ambition [would] counteract ambition" within the federal government, as the "interest of the man [came to be] connected with the constitutional rights of the [branch of government]."[35] But Madison never explained why officials would come to feel an identification with their branch. Even if federal officials did come to experience such institutional loyalties, he did not consider the possibility that they would experience them to different degrees depending upon which branch claimed their allegiance. The lifetime appointments of federal judges and the biennial electoral trials of members of the House of Representatives predictably elicit mentalities with quite different time horizons. These in turn lead to distinct degrees of institutional identification.[36] Neither Madison nor Hamilton reckoned with the possibility that some other supervening motive might sweep across the several branches—uniting what was intended to be distinct.

But within the first decade of the Constitution's creation, the possibility of strong institutional loyalties was swept away by an unexpected, cross-cutting tide: A binary system of national parties had developed around competing ideological poles, and partisan incentives quickly swamped institutional identification. Madison and

Hamilton, with no small irony, played leading roles in the creation of the Jeffersonian Democratic-Republican Party and the Federalist Party, respectively. Hamilton's financial proposals concerning the National Bank and the sinking fund carved a rift in Congress that anticipated and motivated the emerging national party system. Madison and his allies in turn cultivated a network of friendly legislators to resist this centralizing vision of a fiscally empowered national state.

At the same time, geopolitical fissures opened. In France, the blissful first dawn of revolution rhapsodized by radicals from Wordsworth westward gave way to brutal violence as the revolutionaries turned on each other. Disagreement swelled over Washington's 1793 Neutrality Proclamation, and then the Jay Treaty of 1795 with Great Britain, the former colonial overlord. By the time that the voters were asked to choose George Washington's successor, ideological divides had widened to the point that legislators—and presidential candidates—could be clearly identified as Republican or Federalist. Full-scale ideological warfare erupted between John Adams and Thomas Jefferson. It would culminate in the bitter and protracted contestation of the 1800 election. The system of separated powers animated by institutional loyalties anticipated by the Framers was by then moribund, substantially ousted by the separation between national political parties.[37]

The existence and ensuing strength of partisan motives since 1800 is plainly at odds with Hamilton's assumption of a stable, steady-state equilibrium between the Senate and the presidency. Working within the same powerful field of partisan forces as the White House, the Senate will not act as a consistent constraint on presidential choices. Senators are more likely to respond to partisan motives rather than institutional ones because they anticipate elections in which they must justify their record to retain office. Before the Seventeenth Amendment was enacted in 1913, to be sure, senators could be selected by their home state's legislature rather than being elected. But this hardly insulated them from partisan forces. Ideological conflict within the statehouses was so great that in the 1850s Indiana went without a senator for two years. Between 1899 and 1903 Delaware likewise went short in the Senate because of disabling internal conflict between different political factions. The Madisonian model of "filtration" through state legislators, in other words, was thwarted by partisan forces both before and after the Seventeenth Amendment.

As a result of separation by party rather than branch, the behavior of the Senate would come to turn on the balance of partisan forces across the nation. More specifically, it would depend on which states' delegates could cast a pivotal vote on a judicial nomination. During periods of unified government, when the Senate and the presidency were aligned, a controlling block of senators would not withhold cooperation with the White House, or even screen closely presidential appointments. But when the Senate was in hostile hands, the Senator casting a controlling vote would likely have powerful reasons to block presidential appointments, or to limit the range of feasible appointments. She or he would likely to act for partisan advantage rather than out of public-spirited, good-governance motives. Of course, there could be instances in which partisan motives will lead the Senate to approve worthy nominees by a president from the opposing party and to block unworthy ones from their own side. The greater the overlap between the parties' overall range of policy preferences, the more likely this is to happen.

The persistence of partisan polarization to varying degrees through US history does not defeat the possibility of the Senate working as a failsafe against poor presidential choices. It does not rule out, that is, periods of cooperation and partisan comity over judicial appointments. It suggests instead that Hamilton's device is more vulnerable to failure under conditions of greater polarization within the Senate. When polarization is great, divided government will often lead to a breakdown in judicial appointments, whereas unified government will generally lead to those appointments being made without any kind of substantive Senate check.

Hence, senators today routinely block, or "blue slip," ideologically distant nominees to the lower courts even when they are highly qualified.[38] When they cannot entirely block a nominee, senators search for ways to delay a nomination, perhaps buying time for a new president to enter the White House. While the Senate's refusal to hold hearings or vote upon President Obama's nomination of Merrick Garland to the Supreme Court is the most notorious example of this, there is a long history of senatorial delays of judicial nominees for partisan purposes.[39]

A rational president, in anticipation of such patterns of strategic and partisan behavior by the Senate, will not put forward nominations to a hostile body when there is a chance of a more receptive audience somewhere down the road. Judicial appointments, as a result, will come in waves, as presidents take advantage of their fellow partisans' victory in Senate elections, or alternatively bide their time, waiting for a better day. Once judges are appointed with clear ideological preferences, moreover, they will have every reason to hold onto their seats to the maximal extent possible, at least until an aligned president is in office. Judges who can decide on their retirement date, including Supreme Court appointees, also have good cause to behave strategically to preserve their party's hold on a court (although this can misfire if the jurist miscalculates her window of opportunity). The net result of these dynamics is a vicious circle—with ideological patterns of judicial appointment begetting later strategic judicial behavior by judges and yet more ideologically polarized appointments by presidents. Rather than tamping down on partisan incentives, or generating a steady-state equilibrium in which well-qualified candidates with relatively weak partisan motives reach the bench, the

Constitution's design accelerates the pace and intensity of partisan competition over the judiciary. This is so especially under conditions of partisan polarization. Article III hence serves to sharpen, not blunt, the penetration of the federal bench by partisan conflict precisely at the moment such warfare will be most bitter.

Few today can deny that the force of partisan identification has increased rather than decreased in the last few decades, raising anew barriers to a Madisonian dynamic in the separation of powers. The political scientist Lee Drutman has argued that the repulsive force of partisan polarization is on the rise thanks to recent changes to the structure of national politics. While a two-party structure was manifest in national politics even in the 1790s, he argues, until recently the two parties were "capacious, incoherent, and overlapping" because of cross-cutting regional affiliations. Since the 1980s, however, there has been a sharp polarization among political elites. A downstream consequence of this is a purging of tensions and impurities from the two main national parties. Drutman persuasively argues that partisan polarization was always latent in the constitutional design, but that late-twentieth-century developments have dramatically increased its salience and force.[40] If, therefore, the Senate-presidency equilibrium was imperiled in the 1790s, there is every reason to anticipate that it will be dead by the late 2020s.

Polarization interacts with another element of the Senate's design to influence judicial appointment. Representation in the Senate is by state rather than by population. When a party caucus controlling the Senate comprises more members from smaller and less populous states, a demographic minority of the country will have a decisive voice in judicial appointments. Where a president wins office without winning the popular vote, aligned with a winning majority in the Senate that reflects a minority of the country, judicial appointments will tend to reflect the preferences of a demographic minority.[41]

Another of Hamilton's assumptions was that the bar would remain a closely held preserve of the learned few. This too started to erode in the decade following the Constitution's adoption. In Litchfield, Connecticut, Federalist lawyer Tapping Reeve and his associate James Gould found themselves with a large number of law apprentices. Reeve turned his attention away from client service and toward educating this cadre of budding legal professionals for the new Republic. Litchfield had declined as a law school by the 1820s, but by then other schools had emerged, such as Yale and Harvard. This new market in legal education increased the availability of lawyers, particularly elite lawyers, by supplementing the then-dominant source of legal talent coming from law-office apprenticeships. Through the nineteenth century, apprenticed lawyers such as Abraham Lincoln continued to play important roles in public life.[42] As late as 1941, a lawyer who had never matriculated from law school, Robert Jackson, could be appointed to the Supreme Court. While it is technically possible for a nonlawyer to be appointed to the Court today, the conventions and expectations surrounding appointment make this very unlikely to happen.

The growth of pathways to the bar for lawyers both plebian and elite undermined Hamilton's assumption that the president and the Senate would have little choice but to appoint those extremely learned in the law. Today, Hamilton's argument from scarcity plainly no longer holds. There are more than enough men—and, happily, women, transgender, and nonbinary individuals—trained in the law to staff the judiciary. Accounting for the range of students attending various law schools, the eligible population as a whole is also ideologically heterogeneous. Law students may be predictably uniform along some margins, but they are not clustered uniquely at one single pole of today's polarized political landscape. As a result, judges who wish to hire recent graduates as law clerks but who want to hire only ideologically sympathetic students can and do find kindred spirits regardless of where they stand on the political spectrum.[43]

In light of the democratization of the legal profession, it is implausible to assume that supply-side constraints will again work as effective determinants of judicial independence. Indeed, this was so evident that by 1970 Senator Roman Hruska could complain, apropos the failed nomination of G. Harrold Carswell to the Supreme Court, that "there are a lot of mediocre judges and people and lawyers. They are entitled to a little representation, aren't they?"[44] So much, then, for the idea of supply-side constraints preventing the politicization of the judiciary.

Finally, it would be unwise to look to substantive federal law as a constraint on judicial discretion. In large part, this is because of the increasing complexity of the national economy that Hamilton worked so hard to build. That growing economy has increased the volume and complexity of federal legislation needed to keep goods and services in motion. The ensuing increase in the volume in legislation created new opportunities for laws to come into conflict with each other. It has also vastly amplified the range of possible conflicts with the capaciously drafted and ambiguous provisions of the federal Constitution. Whereas at the beginning of the Republic, few provisions of the Constitution were understood to be appropriate for judicial application, over time the sheer range of potential grounds for a constitutional challenge has grown. This growth was especially rapid after the Civil War of the 1860s.[45] The rapid proliferation of textual grounds for a judge's intervention into politics—including different federal statutes and various elements of the Constitution's text—has not served to constrain judicial discretion. Quite the opposite. Because many difficult cases will present a plurality of possible rationales, judges enjoy a degree of freedom that they lacked in the early Republic.

By the early twentieth century, the very idea that constitutional or statutory texts would always supply fixed and determinate answers to legal questions came to be severely doubted. A movement in the legal academy called "legal realism," broadly aligned with progressive policy goals, challenged this notion. Legal realism arose at a time when leading judges hewed to a formalist style of reasoning to reach generally conservative and economically regressive outcomes.[46] But its insights are more general in scope. The belief that judges can always mine the written materials of law to isolate one single "right" answer in hard cases, that evaluations of normative and empirical questions play no role in that enterprise, and that juristic skill will necessarily discipline their discretion in that enterprise— all this seems an artifact of history.

The argument for the constraining force of substantive law also assumes that Congress has an incentive to enact clear laws. But this premise has also come unmoored. Once again, the reason is a rise in partisan disagreement. Legislators from different parties often agree that a policy problem exists but disagree about how to solve it. Both sides want to enact legislation, claim credit, and avoid criticism from their partisan supporters. One way to do this is to enact vague statutes that allow both sides to trumpet their victory in solving a problem. Vagueness in statutory text allows legislators to assert their ongoing fidelity to ideological priors, and—even better—to later jawbone the executive branch to get the law enforced in the way they want. The incentive to defer substantive choices from the time of a law's enactment to the time of its implementation is exacerbated by the sheer number of vetoes wielded by legislators in committees, on the floor of a House, and in the reconciliation process.[47] These "vetogates" make it more difficult for legislators to converge on specific text. Instead, they are pushed by Congress's structure to leave matters to the executive, or alternatively to treat courts as "dumping grounds" for hot-button issues that are too divisive for legislative coalitions to resolve.[48] This interaction between the Constitution's design and the unanticipated currents of partisan competition pushes legislators toward vague or ambiguous statutory language that places little constraint on judicial discretion.

OPEN VEINS OF POLITICAL INFLUENCE IN THE FEDERAL JUDICIARY

The Constitution is a victim of its own success. The design of Article III courts in particular was premised on assumptions about the manner in which novel national institutions would interact with each other, and also with abiding social and political forces in the wider nation. The mechanisms underpinning judicial independence rest on the putative strength of institutional loyalties and the ability of social and professional forces to elicit a professional, legalistic, and nonpartisan bench. Thanks in part to its own ideological architects, Hamilton and Madison, the Constitution succeeded in unleashing social, ideological, and economic forces that would wash these presuppositions away. Article III's reliance on ex post, individually focused mechanisms to create judicial independence became a victim of the Constitution's more general success in precipitating a new kind of national politics characterized by two national parties, as well as its success in creating a national economy that would support far more than a handful of lawyers. The collapse of Article III's assumptions, in other words, is a signal of the success of other elements of the constitutional design.

The legacy of the Article III blueprint for constitutional remedies must thus be understood in light of complex social and political dynamics. To read it as a mere text in isolation from these currents is to invite error. The Constitution created a judiciary that lacked effectual means for exercising power against other branches or even for self-protection. How could it prevent other state actors from infringing on individual negative rights? And even if that blueprint had created an effectually independent tribunal, the Madisonian theory of the separation of powers left open a puzzle: A theory of "institutional loyalties" presupposes a set of distinctively institutional interests to be pursued. But even if it could wriggle free of the elected branches' influences, what exactly would the judiciary want? It was a question that would not be fully asked and answered for almost a century and a half, just as the courts were in the process of developing as potential guardians of individual rights.

CHAPTER 2

Building

Throughout this vast republic, from the St. Croix to the Gulf of Mexico, from the Atlantic to the Pacific, revenue is to be collected and expended, armies are to be marched and supported. . . . Is that construction of the constitution to be preferred, which would render these operations difficult, hazardous and expensive?

Chief Justice John Marshall[1]

IN JANUARY 1801, a British merchant named John Laird filed a suit in a Virginia federal court demanding that a federal marshal force the sale of property belonging to a Virginian merchant, Hugh Stuart, for unpaid debts. Unwittingly, Laird thereby set in motion one of the most important—and certainly the most overlooked—opinion published by the early American judiciary. That opinion tells clearly the consequences of the failed assumptions of Article III. It sets the stage for the path taken by federal courts across the nineteenth and early twentieth centuries. And it reveals just how fragile and evanescent the Article III model of judicial independence would prove to be.

Little is known about what happened in the run-up to and during the early stages of the *Stuart v. Laird* litigation.[2] We do know that Laird prevailed at first in the fourth federal circuit court, which sat in Richmond. We also know that he obtained a remedy called a "writ of fieri facias," a document issued by a court that allowed a creditor to "execute" a debt by seizing some of the debtors' goods. The reply to that writ stated that it was to be "Executed on Maria and child, Paul, Jenny, Selah, Kate, and Anna, and a bond taken with Charles L. Carter security, for the delivery thereof at the Eagle tavern, in the city of Richmond, on the 20th day of April, 1802, the condition of which was not complied with." The record doesn't tell us more about who Maria and the others were. But the Eagle Tavern was one of the main sites for the auction of enslaved persons in Richmond, and it is unlikely that an indentured servant could have served as a security for a debt. So it is hard to shake the suspicion that the security for Stuart's debt was a group of human beings in chains. Laird, in any event, seems not to have secured the remedy that he most wanted, and so went back to federal court. Here he ran into a serious problem: The fourth circuit court that had issued the initial execution writ no longer existed. It had been abolished by legislative fiat in April 1802, its judges shorn of their Article III robes. Congress had replaced it with the fifth circuit court. And when Laird sought to press his claims in this new court, Stuart objected that the fourth circuit that had issued the initial writ no longer existed. Although his argument is not wholly clear, it seems to rest on the claim that Congress lacked the power to abolish that court or to transfer its caseload to a new forum. Defending his property in Maria, Paul, and the others, Stuart raised a question about the metes and bounds of Article III.

The fourth circuit court, where Laird had originally filed, had sprung to life on February 13, 1801. It was the result of a comprehensive rout of John Adams's Federalist Party in the 1800 elections. The

Federalists lost the White House and Congress. Rather than accept defeat with grace, the lame-duck Federalists scrambled to entrench their fading political authority against the impinging Jeffersonian tide. Among the redoubts into which they scrambled was the federal judiciary. The February 1801 Judiciary Act, passed by that lame-duck Federalist Congress, seeded sixteen new judgeships and six new permanent intermediate, or circuit, courts.[3] This filled a gap in the judicial system drawn up in 1789 by Oliver Ellsworth, which had created trial courts and the Supreme Court, but did not provide for any permanent or fixed intermediate courts of appeal. It was in one of these new circuit courts that Laird had filed first.

In 1802, the newly empowered Jeffersonian coalition in Congress and the White House responded to the Federalists' last-minute ploy by simply abolishing the new circuit courts and letting go the sixteen new federal judges employed to staff them.[4] Cases such as Laird's were moved to other, preexisting tribunals. But as Stuart's attorney Mr. Lee pointed out, even if Congress might have the power to decide which federal courts existed, firing federal judges in the process, it could not simply remove judges who had comported with the Constitution's "good behavior" rule. Surely, Mr. Lee contended, that "excellent barrier to the encroachments and oppressions of the representative body" could not be so easily and quickly circumvented?"[5]

But Mr. Lee's argument found no receptive audience in the halls of federal justice. Whatever institutional loyalties Madison anticipated were mere fumes in the heat of actual conflict. In a first-round hearing, Chief Justice John Marshall dismissed Stuart's plea, and he recused himself when the matter went to the Supreme Court. There, Justice William Paterson wrote a terse and evasive opinion deflecting any Article III concern. The Court imposed no limit on Congress's control of the institutional elements of jurisdiction and court structure. It described no constraint upon legislators' use of these powers as a means of undermining the individual-level devices of tenure and salary protection. The sixteen judges who lost their positions fared no better. Deprived of their Article III commissions, these judges considered a lawsuit. They decided instead to approach the House and the Senate, cap in hand, for the balance of their salaries on the bench. They had no success.[6] We do not know what happened to Maria, Paul, Jenny, Selah, Kate, and Anna.

Stuart was decided just six days after the more famous *Marbury v. Madison* case. The *Marbury* opinion is now perceived as having established the power of federal courts to review the constitutionality of, and if necessary strike down, federal statutes.[7] While *Marbury* has taken on a canonical tincture, the constitutional law casebooks that most law students use today scarcely mention *Stuart*. If it is cited at all, it is only in passing. The decision does not fit with today's celebratory narrative of an inevitably ascendant judicial power, one measured by the Supreme Court's ever-more aggressive exercise of constitutional review. But the *Stuart* decision captures more accurately than *Marbury* the precarious position in which federal courts found themselves after the failure of Article III's presuppositions. It positions us to see how partisan control of jurisdiction and staffing have shaped federal judicial power—and it helps us perceive the ways in which the judiciary more generally has been put to the service of a larger project of building a new American state. Only when that state-building project took off, after the Civil War, did an opportunity arise for the judiciary to seize a real measure of institutional autonomy.

Stuart was not a ticket good for one ride only. In 1812, Congress admitted Louisiana as a state of the union. In so doing, it eliminated first the federal district court that had been created in 1804 for that territory, and then created a new district court. This time, no one lost their job: The territorial judge secured the new judgeship created by the statehood act. In 1862, Congress reorganized the District of Columbia courts, abolishing three judgeships without reappointing those who lost their positions.[8] Finally, in 1913, Congress abolished the three-year-old Commerce Court, which had been staffed with federal judges, reappointing all but one to other federal courts. The one who was not reappointed, to be fair, had been impeached on grounds of bribery in the meanwhile.[9]

This chapter traces two dynamics that shaped the translation from the Article III blueprint to actual institutions through the nineteenth and early twentieth centuries. The first is the porous interface between the courts and the political branches left by the failure of Alexander Hamilton's assumptions of interbranch separation. Throughout the nineteenth century, federal courts were employed by elected coalitions as key elements of various state-building projects pursued by national political coalitions. Because the national state of the nineteenth century was relatively fragile, however, the potential reach of its courts was also constrained. Theirs is a story of institutional dependence, and of the subservience of legal institutions to transient political ends.

The second dynamic arose later, after the Civil War, as the national state began to thicken and flex its muscles. In this context, coalitions of partisan elected officials decided to lean on the federal courts to pursue national policy agendas that direct legislative or executive action could not easily achieve. Thanks to entrepreneurial and savvy Chief Justices, the judiciary secured a measure of freedom to pursue its own interests while furthering these partisan agendas. To understand the judiciary's role in the larger tapestry of American state activity, and its ambivalence about the defense of individual rights, both of these dynamics demand attention. Today, judicial power remains an unstable blend of vulnerability to partisan ideological shifts colliding with, leveraging, or undermining institutional loyalties. The current condition of constitutional remedies is a product of these forces.

To trace the growth of the federal courts as a partisan-fueled project intertwined in the larger project of American state-building, and to locate the buds of judicial autonomy after the Civil War, is to rub against the grain of traditional, Whiggish constitutional history. A more familiar story is centered on the Supreme Court. It starts with *Marbury* establishing the power of judicial review and proceeds through a greatest hits of constitutional precedent. I skirt those familiar landmarks of Supreme Court history. I also have little to say about the way in which the Supreme Court acquired and legitimated the power to issue general, binding rulings as to the Constitution's meaning. Rather than focusing on the authority of the Court as constitutional interpreter, I am concerned here with the institutional capacity of the federal courts at large to deliver specific outcomes to particular litigants. That institutional history is a reflection, sometimes through a foggy lens, of the Article III blueprint, and of the accumulated political histories through which the scramble for constitutional remedies has unfolded over time.

THE FEDERAL COURTS AND THE PROJECT
OF STATE-BUILDING

The federal courts are an arm of the national state. What sort of role courts can play in the polity depends on the nature of that state. A tension lies at the origins of the American state-building project, clouding what precisely the nation-state will be. On the one hand, the Revolution manifestly repudiated the idea of a concentrated and centralizing state, more common in Europe, that could successfully penetrate into and control society. Following the examples of early American state constitutions, the Articles of Confederation envisaged a weak, infrastructure-poor national government that was highly dependent on its constituent states for funds and arms. It would have been at least possible for the new Constitution to persist on that path. On the other hand, the 1787 Constitution also allowed for the possibility of a far more robust central state apparatus. As Chief Justice Marshall intimated in this chapter's epigraph, the Constitution entertains the possibility of a continent-spanning nation with an economy, a government, and a jackboot to match. During the Convention and the ratification debates, those on the Federalist side made the case for a robust fiscal capacity, in particular supported by the federal government's power to borrow, as a prerequisite to effective military action.[10] The nation-state circa 1787 did not have a predetermined form. For decades, its contours remained the object of abiding, frankly partisan contestation.

As we have seen, Article III gave Congress control of how and when the federal courts would expand. In the antebellum era, legislators did grow those courts when doing so conduced to their immediate state-building ambitions. Yet legislators were also willing to narrow judicial power when doing so advanced these same ambitions. Through the Civil War, the institutional judiciary remained a relatively weak actor, a distinctly second-rate branch in the shadow of Congress and the presidency alike. In the antebellum era, the 1791 Bill of Rights was understood to limit the federal government but not the states. Congress, though, did not see fit to use the federal courts to vindicate federal rights, with important and telling exceptions such as the Fugitive Slave Act of 1850. As a result, the federal courts were in no position to engage in the robust definition or defense of federal or constitutional rights. To the extent that they were able to pursue the vindication of individual rights, their action was an interstitial and unexpected result of their so-called diversity jurisdiction over suits between citizens of different states. Although the results of these interventions in favor of federal constitutional rights were not entirely inconsequential, the federal courts' deep entanglement in the antebellum project of state-building all but guaranteed that the defense of rights was a relatively minor part of their dockets.

From the very beginning of the Republic, then, the federal judiciary that emerged from the minimal constitutional blueprint was a product of fierce partisan competition over the nature of the state. At its inception, the first organic statute creating federal courts ex nihilo in 1789 responded to conflicts between creditors such as Laird on the one hand, and the state legislators and judges who tended to be more sensitive to co-citizen debtors such as Stuart. It was drafted by a Connecticut Yankee, Senator Oliver Ellsworth, known to be sympathetic to the creditors' cause. Many of these lenders, like Laird, were British. The Scottish town of Glasgow, where Laird seemed to have been based, enjoyed the advantage of a quicker voyage to the Chesapeake Bay in contrast to more southerly-based merchants. The result was a booming, debt-financed trade tacking forth from the Clyde to the new American nation. By the beginning of the Revolutionary War, for example, the Glasgow merchant William Cunninghame was owed the then-fantastical sum of 135,000 pounds by Maryland and Virginia yeoman farmers. Slave markets such as the Eagle Tavern and its ilk likely did a brisk trade.[11] Yet after the Revolutionary War, numerous states created new barriers to relief sought by creditors in state court, limiting interest and requiring delayed repayments, and even, in the case of South Carolina, closing its courts to certain creditors entirely.[12]

Against this backdrop, Ellsworth's legislative schema for a new federal judiciary created a three-tiered system of courts, with permanent district (trial) courts and a Supreme Court. It also imagined an intermediate level of "circuit" panels, but did not imagine that these would have judges permanently assigned to them. Instead, they would be staffed them with district judges and Supreme Court Justices. Importantly, Ellsworth's draft gave those circuit panels power to hear "diversity" cases, which pitted the inhabitants of different states against each other. Diversity cases included many of the creditor-debtor suits that had motivated Ellsworth and others, including Laird, to work toward a national judiciary. In contrast, Ellsworth did not give the new national courts power to hear cases simply because they presented a federal question of law. This gap reflected continuing anxiety about the federal courts as potential competition for state courts. A Pennsylvania senator grumbled that new national courts would, if unchecked, "swallow all the State constitutions by degree."[13] The absence of federal-question jurisdiction meant that the state courts would necessarily be the first to hear many issues about the new Constitution and the laws enacted by the new Congress.

As a result, the lower federal judiciary created in 1789 was nothing like the robust and extensive institution of today. It was made up of a modest system of thirteen district courts and three circuit courts. Per Ellsworth's design, the latter were staffed by Justices and district-court judges, and lacked their own dedicated personnel. Most states hence had only one federal trial judge. These judges would hear diversity matters, maritime cases, and some cases involving penalties and forfeitures under the laws of the United States. No cases came before them simply because an individual constitutional right had been violated. Nor were things much different at the top. When the Supreme Court first met in February 1790 in New York, it was a "sorry scene," with only four of six Justices bothering to show up and not a single case in sight.[14] The Justices had to "ride circuit," which involved treacherous and tiring journeys across the country to decide what Chief Justice William Rehnquist would later call "dull and uninteresting" disputes over the technicalities of states' procedural rules and the state common-law rules for torts, contracts, land titling, and jury instruction.[15] Hardly the stuff of judicial heroics.

The 1789 plan for the judiciary reflected congressional priorities about the division of labor between the federal government and the several states. It also implicitly embodied a view about how far the new national state could or should extend. At the time of the 1789 Judiciary Act's passage, then–Chief Justice John Jay worried about the system's "difficulties" and predicted that federal judges would be repeatedly "embarrassed" given the difficulty that the federal government would have enforcing its writ across the new nation.[16] The ultimately failed Federalist effort to expand the federal courts in 1801 also reflected long-simmering grievances about the proper scope of federal judicial power and the nature of the state. In addition to advancing the Federalists' prophylactic partisan ambitions, the 1801 Act served their policy agenda of a more powerful federal judiciary. It added "federal question" jurisdiction to the diversity jurisdiction already created in 1798. The 1801 Act also evinced their judgment that a system of lower federal courts should symbolize and embody the authority of the general, national government in each far-flung corner of the newly extended republic.[17] Which is all to say that it did all this for the brief year in which it was good law.

Had the Federalist jurisdictional plan of 1801 succeeded, the lower courts might well have been transformed into one of the most prominent vectors of early national authority. In the early Republic, the main armatures of federal power into the daily lives of Americans were the customs service (at least in ports) and the post office. Through the 1790s, Congress repeatedly took up legislation to extend and enable the postal service to nurse into being a national sphere of political debate.[18] In the Jeffersonian and early Jacksonian era, Congress then found itself roiled by complex constitutional debates over whether the general government could fund "internal improvements" such as roads and canals necessary for the postal system to prosper.[19] Federal and state efforts to cajole, bribe, or coerce Indigenous peoples from their ancestral lands separately produced a set of legal debates about the nature of treaty rights, the origins of property, and the balance of power between the federal government and the states. Federal courts endorsed the settler property rights created through a slow and insidious process of "Indian removal." Judges' occasional qualms proved futile and in any case fleeting.[20] Setting to one side the ensuing, highly successful campaign of ethnic cleansing that followed,[21] antebellum development of an effectual national state was halting, reluctant, and partial right through to the Civil War.

The path of subsequent legislation modifying the federal courts also tells of the subservience of federal judicial power to the larger project of American state-building. It was in response to the westward expansion of the United States that an 1807 act added a new circuit court for the western states of Kentucky, Tennessee, and Ohio. These would otherwise have been excluded from the circuit system.[22] A persisting lag between western expansion and the extension of the circuit-court system nevertheless was to occasion continued "vexation and distress" until the enactment of the Judiciary Act of 1837.[23] Under this act, nine circuits were created, and the Supreme Court was expanded to its now-familiar size of nine. Each Justice was assigned to a specific circuit. Five of the nine circuits sat in slave states, a reflection of the contemporaneous sectional balance of power. The act also allowed Andrew Jackson to make his sixth Supreme Court appointment out of eight Justices then sitting on the court. The failure of Hamilton's anticipated balance between the president and the Senate meant that these appointments were made on the basis of the partisan priorities of the Jacksonian system at large. As a result of all this legislation and these appointments, the vigorously proslavery class of Jackson-appointed Justices would go on to serve a combined 138 years on the bench. They continued to shape federal law through the Civil War. Hence, much like its predecessors, the 1837 Act reflected the partisan imperatives of its age—and did so in ways that would embody, and hence perpetuate, the antebellum settlement of the slavery question.[24]

Yet neither the 1807 nor the 1837 Acts nor the miscellany of other, more ministerial, statutes passed in the latter's wake fundamentally changed the capacity of the federal courts. The fragile judicial system of the 1790s, with little ability to supervise the conduct of either state or federal actors, remained relatively weak right until the Civil War. Nothing was more emblematic of this weakness than the inefficacy of the "paper victory" the Supreme Court gave to the Cherokee against removal by Georgia authorities, a ruling that gave Indigenous peoples little shelter from state violence.[25] This profound institutional weakness rendered implausible the very idea of systematic judicial resistance to rights violations inflicted on socially marginal groups, particularly by the federal government.

The same was true of the federal bench's relationship to the states. When the Justices declared in 1833 that the 1791 Bill of Rights applied only against the federal government and not the states, its decision can be understood as a flag of institutional weakness as much as evidence of its jurisprudential acuity.[26] That 1833 decision also meant that the state judiciary had relatively few opportunities to enforce federal rules against state officials for the simple reason that when a state official used coercion, he was usually unconstrained by the Constitution. Nor did state courts play a large role in checking federal government action under the Bill of Rights. In a smattering of instances, a state court would resist federal action. Prior to the Civil War, for example, state courts did occasionally issue the writ of habeas corpus as relief against unlawful federal detention for the purpose of conscription.[27] Very rarely, a state court would invalidate a federal statute. In 1863, for example, the Supreme Court of Indiana invalidated one of the federal indemnification acts passed to limit federal exposure to damages claims during the Civil War.[28] But these state judicial interventions against national power were relatively infrequent. Hamilton's expectation that the state governments would be "the immediate and visible guardian of life and property" was simply not borne out, at least when it came to constitutional violations being redressed through the courts.[29]

Rather than a source of constraint on government, the role of the federal courts in this period is better understood in terms of the assistance they lent—albeit occasionally, and not necessarily to great effect—to the project of building a national state. In the late 1830s, for example, states came to rely on the promulgation of specialized corporate charters to promote economic development. Glossing the scope and meaning of these charters fell to the courts. Federal judges as a result became "the chief source of economic surveillance in the nineteenth century." Just as the federal courts of the 1790s were conceived as instruments for protecting the interests of capital in the form of creditors, foreign and domestic, so the judicial interpretation of corporate charters of the mid-nineteenth century bent toward "predictable but flexible forms of policy" enabling capital accumulation.[30] Not individual rights per se, but rather commerce, and hence the protection of the first shoots of an newly emergent capitalist system, provided a touchstone for the early, ambitious exercise of judicial power.

EMBERS OF INDIVIDUAL RIGHTS IN THE EARLY REPUBLIC

Nevertheless, there were suggestive hints in the antebellum period of the judiciary's capacity to play a more robust role in vindicating individuals' rights against the state. Three threads of federal court case law are worth drawing out. These complicate the story of federal courts as mere handmaidens of aggressive state-building. Different kinds of rights are at stake in each strand. Together they provide subtle hints about the role that federal courts would come to play with respect to individual rights at the end of the nineteenth century and in the twentieth century.

First, where the federal courts did have jurisdiction, they proved occasionally willing to sanction national government officials for discrete acts of malfeasance. One of the domains in which early federal courts exercised broad jurisdiction and could vindicate what look like individual rights involved maritime matters. Another is the scattering of cases that arose out of the War of 1812.[31] In the maritime context of admiralty jurisdiction, courts could be faced with the claim that a government official had seized a ship, or the goods carried on it, without lawful authority. In the war cases, the federal courts might be asked to free someone who had been improperly detained.

In a case that made it all the way to the Supreme Court, a merchant named Mr. Barreme filed an action against US Navy Captain George Little for the improper (and hence unlawful) seizure of the Danish vessel the *Flying Fish*. Captaining the USS *Boston*, Little had seized the Flying Fish near Haiti for unlawfully trading with the French. Writing for the Supreme Court, Chief Justice John Marshall found that Little's action fell outside the scope of seizures that Congress had authorized—and thus warranted an award of damages to Barreme amounting to $8,504.[32]

Such a finding did not contradict Congress's wishes. To the contrary, as early as 1802, Congress had enacted indemnification measures for unlawful seizures, allowing defendants such as Little to obtain shelter from court-imposed financial exposure. Its actions, however, were not entirely altruistic. President Jefferson was at the time pursuing a policy of neutrality with France, urging respect for the rights of neutral vessels, and seeking indemnification for unlawfully seized American vessels. The Danish demand for compensation was also backed by diplomatic pressure upon then–secretary of state James Madison. Geopolitical considerations related to the maintenance of peaceful relations and international trade, in short, helped along Mr. Barreme's case.[33] Litigation that seemed to pivot around the protection of individual rights would, not for the last time, advance because of geopolitical imperatives. Today, legal scholars look back to these cases, quite reasonably, as evidence of how the federal courts can play a remedial role protecting individual rights. But it is worth remembering that these decisions arose in one of the few domains in which Congress had given federal judges jurisdictional leeway—maritime cases. And without this jurisdictional license in the first place, the *Flying Fish* case would have floundered.

Second, federal courts used diversity jurisdiction imaginatively as a vessel by which to protect the interests of out-of-state actors under the Contract Clause of the US Constitution. In the nineteenth century, explained Justice George Shiras, "No provision of the Constitution of the United States . . . received more frequent consideration."[34] These diversity cases braided together the protection of constitutional rights with the more general orientation of the federal courts toward the protection and vindication of an emergent form of capitalism. The Contract Clause was deployed to invalidate state laws found to interfere with tax-exemption agreements, corporate charters, land grants, and agreements between states. It was also applied to rein in debtor relief laws and profligate states' efforts to repudiate their own bonds.[35] Although the lower federal courts could not hear a case on the sole ground that it implicated a Contract Clause question, they stretched the bounds of diversity jurisdiction with the ill-disguised purpose of reaching and deciding a federal constitutional question.[36] In this way, ordinary private law disputes involving trespass and contract could be alchemized by federal judges into new constitutional rules.

For example, in the 1855 case of *Dodge v. Woolsey*, an out-of-state shareholder sued an Ohio official to stop him from collecting a tax higher than the bank's corporate charter allowed. Under the Court's long-standing case law, diversity jurisdiction should not have existed because a company's shareholders were conclusively presumed to live in the entity's state of incorporation (Ohio). The dispute should have been dismissed for want of jurisdiction. But the Court instead flagged the "large pecuniary interest" that the plaintiff had in the bank. It celebrated, in a long, sententious, and rather disingenuous disquisition, the "higher aim and purpose" of diversity jurisdiction to "make the people think and feel, though residing in different States of the Union, that their relations to each other were protected by the strictest justice." Then it made short work of the actual tax increase—striking it down under a rule established in earlier precedent.[37]

Cases such as *Woolsey* were also of a piece with another series of decisions in which the Supreme Court reviewed the work of a state court, and then reversed on the ground that a state-law remedy for a constitutional rights violation was inadequate. As in *Woolsey*, the rights claimants in these cases were typically (if not always) corporate actors bucking state regulation.[38] At the very general level of public policy, all of these cases hence ran on a similar ideological track to the design of the 1787 Judiciary Act and its successors in favor of interstate markets and national commercial interests. As in the *Flying Fish* case, the claimant to a constitutional right tended to be a member of the entrepreneurial and mercantile class. It was, again, the creditor (this time unsecured) and domiciled outside the state in which the action unfolded who looked to the federal courts. Again, he found succor in that forum. If there was a distributive lilt in these cases, it spoke in an accent ringing with dollars.

There is a third and final domain in which Congress conscripted the federal courts into the defense of rights in the Republic's early years. The right at stake was the property interest in human beings created by the American law of slavery. Properly viewed as abhorrent now, the federal fugitive slave laws nevertheless are instructive today. They illustrate both political control over federal-court jurisdiction being deployed to vindicate "rights," albeit of an odious sort, and also the limits of that strategy for the rights holders in the absence of a strong national state.

The first Fugitive Slave Act, enacted after tortuous debate in Congress in 1793, allowed the putative owners of slaves to travel to the north to recapture "their" slaves and bring them before a state or federal judge, justice of the peace, or magistrate. These officials could issue certificates of removal upon determining that the person seized was indeed the claimant's property.[39] In operation, the law yielded ambiguous results. Often, court costs, attorney's fees, and the burden of travel to and from a free state would exceed a slave's pecuniary value. This made recourse to the law economically unattractive. Northern states, moreover, enacted "personal liberty laws" designed to prevent kidnapping of Black people. These in practice hindered unlawful and lawful claims to slave property alike. As a result, the 1793 law had by 1830 become "virtually unenforceable" outside states bordering the Mason-Dixon line or the Ohio River, as well as in New York City.[40] Still, there were *some* cases in which slaveholders successfully called on federal courts for aid in their pursuit of escaped "property." In the spring of 1842, a man named John Van Zandt encountered a group of nine fleeing slaves and hid them in his covered wagon. While the slave owner ultimately recovered all but one of the slaves, he nevertheless went on to sue Van Zandt under the Fugitive Slave Act for damages totaling twelve hundred dollars. The case went to the US Supreme Court, with Van Zandt ably represented by the future Supreme Court Chief Justice Salmon P. Chase. Without dissent, the Court ruled against Van Zandt.[41]

Even if the federal courts proved of limited use in retrieving specific slaves, at the apex the Supreme Court offered slaveholders helpful interpretations of federal law. In 1842, most importantly, the Court in a case called *Prigg v. Pennsylvania* emphatically upheld the constitutionality of the 1793 Act and invalidated northern states' personal liberty laws as improper interferences in the federal mission of slave rendition. At the same time, *Prigg* suggested that active state cooperation with the federal recovery of slaves was a moral rather than a legal duty—such that state officials could but didn't have to collaborate even if they could not stand in the way. But doing so did little to mitigate the damage the *Prigg* decision had otherwise inflicted.[42] The net result of these laws and decisions was that "slavery remained an American rather than a regional or local institution" through the antebellum period.[43]

In 1850, as part of Henry Clay's Compromise, Congress amended the Fugitive Slave Act. Under this new dispensation, a slaveowner had only to produce an affidavit, signed by an officer of a southern court, that described the alleged fugitive and said that he or she was owned by the claimant. Once this was presented to a federal official called a commissioner, the alleged slave could no longer testify on her own behalf, had no access to counsel, and had no right to a public hearing. No appeal from a commissioner's decision was allowed. And the commissioner received a five-dollar fee upon deciding that a Black man, woman, or child was free, but ten dollars if he found the person was a slave.[44] This compensation structure made it clear that the law's bypassing of the federal courts had a singular ambition. In the Senate's debates on the measure, Senator William Dayton of New Jersey had proposed the use of a jury to determine the fugitive's status—only to have the proposal roundly mocked and rejected by the southern states' delegations.[45] The Supreme Court unanimously upheld the law in 1859.[46]

Even in their early fragility, in sum, federal courts did intermittently engage in the protection of individual rights. The rights in play in these cases, however, were not necessarily the individual rights that leap to mind most readily today. They were the rights of those who held property in slaves and ships, or those of creditors with interests in the property of debtors, including the slaves who made up a large share of antebellum capital. While property interests of a sort remain an important part of the network of individual rights widely valued today, it is striking that all of these early cases concern property and contract-based claims being advanced by relatively powerful and economically privileged actors: the owners of vessels engaged in transatlantic trade, shareholders in national banks, and the owners and exploiters of human flesh.

This commonality of position, though, is likely no coincidence. All three strands of jurisprudence participated in a larger project of building a particular kind of national economy. They did so at the behest of parties that benefited most from a certain set of capitalist arrangements—including the enabling of transnational trade, the rise of national finance, and the rejection of Black humanity in service of an agrarian, plantation-based economy. These cases, in other words, do not stand apart from the larger project of American state-building: They resonate with that project by constitutional design. They flowed out of the porous texture of Article III. The resulting judicial mission was a function of legislative judgments about the direction and contours of the American nation-state. Of course, there was often disagreement on the nature of that state-building project. Disagreement would generate the brief jurisdictional expansion and collapse of 1801–1802. It would also lead Congress to dither between 1807 and 1837 before extending the circuit courts westward as the nation rolled on relentlessly. But such disagreement did not give courts a license to act as the elected branches bickered. It was instead disabling. At least through the end of the antebellum period, therefore, the federal courts' reach remained tightly leashed to that larger project of nation building, a subservient status that flowed directly from the elected branches' control over jurisdiction.

Yet once jurisdiction had been granted, federal judges could exercise a measure of creativity. Rights enforcement arises, like crabgrass in the cracks of a sidewalk, as the unintended effect of otherwise unrelated jurisdictional grants. Admiralty and diversity jurisdiction were instruments for facilitating the emergent commercial republic, not means to vindicate individual rights. Congress's purposeful suborning of the federal courts to realize property rights, the 1793 Fugitive Slave Act, was no great success. The sheer cost of federal court access and the ability of other state actors to throw up barriers to its operation gummed up its working. Yet as much as they purport to vindicate "rights" (including to property in human beings), these histories are also evidence of the profound structural weakness of judicial independence as defined by the Article III blueprint: its dependence on political action for the authority to act in the first place.

THE EMERGENCE OF JUDICIAL INDEPENDENCE (OF A SORT)

Until the 1870s, then, the infrastructure of the federal courts remained weak. To be sure, the Supreme Court at its apex was not always an inconsequential actor on the national stage. It had endeavored to step into the various land squabbles in the new Republic, albeit with varying levels of success.[47] Following ratification of the second Fugitive Slave Act, it also intervened in the national debate over slavery in *Dred Scott v. Sanford*, asserting authority to settle the constitutional questions whether Blacks were persons and whether Congress had authority to regulate slavery in the western territories (no and no, said the Court). The *Dred Scott* case was not an unanticipated irruption of a legal id into the national consciousness. To the contrary, legislators and the White House had both previously looked to the Court for a resolution of the grinding sectional conflict over slavery. After the decision, President James Buchanan declared those differences "happily, a matter of but little practical importance," given the obligation of all good citizens to "cheerfully submit" to the Court's decision.[48] That, of course, was not quite how things turned out. Even when the Court's position had some support among elected political elites, the response to *Dred Scott* suggested that it was hardly certain to prevail.

Yet in the 1870s, the federal courts began to secure a greater measure of independence. This occurred because of, and not in spite of, choices by the elected branches. The decisions by transient, sometimes quite ephemeral coalitions to expand judicial autonomy were to prove reasonably durable. Rather than rolling them back, subsequent coalitions of legislators and presidents found it more congenial to turn the judiciary toward their own state-construction projects. As a consequence, in the last quarter of the nineteenth century and the first quarter of the twentieth century, the federal judiciary acquired a breadth of jurisdictional discretion, a depth of institutional infrastructure, and a degree of general, popular legitimacy that rendered it quite distinct from its antebellum precursor. While the change was one of degree and not of kind, it was also large enough to identify this period as the birth of a federal judiciary that can plausibly be characterized, in some respects at least, as independent of the elected branches.

Why then? It was, crucially, a moment at which the national economy emerged utterly transformed from the crucible of industrialization. Between 1859 and 1929, the total manufacturing output of the United States grew by a factor of twenty-eight. Between 1850 and 1900, the percentage of Americans living in cities shot up from 15.3 percent to 39.7 percent. And between 1871 and 1900, some 170,000 miles of railroad were set down. Electrification, the literal rise of the skyscraper, and the emergence of the modern factory system—all this changed the warp and woof of American life with a staggering speed we are apt to underestimate today.[49] Facing both the exigencies of civil war and crosswinds fostered by industrialization, the national state was forced to become something new, something more than a collection of parties and courts. Across the board, it was a period of institutional innovation by the federal government. Green tendrils of bureaucracy dove into the loam of the wider country aiming to knit it into a nation-state with a powerful centralized state apparatus. Varietals included the Bureau of Refugees, Freedmen, and Abandoned Lands (commonly known just as the Freedmen's Bureau), which lasted from 1865 to 1870; the Department of Justice created in 1870; and the Interstate Commerce Commission, formed in 1883 to regulate the railways.

It would have been quite astonishing if the federal judiciary had not been swept up by these paroxysms. Porous to projects of state-building that aroused elected coalitions, and capable of taking some of the policy-making weight off those coalitions, the federal courts did indeed convulse into something quite new. It was the moment, in other words, that Chief Justice John Marshall's 1822 preemptory yet prophetic vision of a "vast republic" of commerce and might, stretching "from the St. Croix to the Gulf of Mexico, from the Atlantic to the Pacific" came to be realized.[50] It was a vision that was to be aided and abetted by the federal courts.

So it was that in the aftermath of the Civil War, the federal courts became a far more important instrument of national policy. First this was so in respect to the reknitting of a national polity after the Civil War, and then in respect to the project of building a post–Industrial Revolution national economy along aggressively free-market lines. Congressional attention to the federal courts ticked up immediately after the war. The postbellum Reconstruction Congresses dominated by Radical Republicans moved to protect freed Black people and to consolidate the political changes wrought by the war. It also fashioned new mechanisms for individuals to challenge discrete constitutional torts and expanded the power of courts to issue "habeas" writs, a procedural mechanism for facilitating the judicial review of a person's imprisonment. All of these steps reflected an understandable impatience with state courts. Judges on those benches, Congress believed, were too hostile to Republican-leaning constituencies to be trusted.[51] The efforts to use the courts to further the goals of Reconstruction, while also advancing constituent service goals, would be hobbled by a secular decline in the political and judicial commitment to Reconstruction's goals during the 1870s and 1880s. Yet, as we shall see, several important remedies remained on the books, largely forgotten—to be revived only in the mid-twentieth century.

Perhaps the most important set of statutes enacted in the Civil War's wake concerned the lower federal courts' jurisdiction to hear and decide new and different sorts of cases. In 1868, Congress liberalized the process by which parties could transfer suits from state to federal court. This procedure, called "removal," was never to matter much to Black civil rights plaintiffs. It ended up being an important tool for other, rather more powerful corporate litigants wanting to escape from a state to a federal court. Then in 1875, Congress would go one step further, making changes that would portend a dramatic shift in the capacity of the federal courts to take effective action. The 1875 law marked a dramatic change in the judiciary's role and powers. As such, it is worth more attention.

Like earlier changes to jurisdiction, the 1875 shift arose out of parochially partisan interests and a more outward-looking project of national state-building. In 1874, the Democrats defeated the incumbent Republicans to capture control of the House in the midterms. Like Adams's Federalists at the beginning of the century, the Republicans responded by looking to the federal courts as a means to hold out against ideological foes. The lame-duck Congress enacted legislation that dramatically enlarged federal court jurisdiction. The Judiciary and Removal Act of 1875 gave federal district courts power to hear cases simply because they concerned a question of federal law. This was the first time such "federal question" jurisdiction had been made available since the Federalists' short-lived experiment with such powers in 1801 and 1802.[52] To facilitate access to federal court, the 1875 act also allowed federal judges to hold a plaintiff in default if he or she tried to prevent a case from being removed from state to federal court. State court clerks who hindered the reassignment of a case from state to federal court could also be prosecuted for a federal misdemeanor with sentences of a year of imprisonment and a one-thousand-dollar fine.

A sign of how important these measures proved is the change in the workload of the federal courts. In the decade after 1876, the number of cases in the lower federal courts where the United States was not a party went from 14,397 to 31,455. There is little evidence, to be clear, that this new burst of federal court activity benefited the former slaves of the Confederate states. The main beneficiaries of this shift were instead a new generation of national corporations, in particular railroads, that sought to use the federal courts to slough off state regulation and supervision. Corporations eagerly seized the opportunity created in 1868 to resist redistributive measures such as midwestern states' so-called Granger Laws. These capped the rates that railroads could charge farmers and passengers, benefiting local interests but curtailing the profits of national corporations. The 1868 removal provision also became a potent tool for corporate interests because it enabled corporations to escape states' Granger enforcement regimes.[53] The law that the late-nineteenth-century federal courts created was the law of transportation, the law of the corporation, and the law of commerce.[54] It was a law to knit together a newly expanding commercial and industrial republic quite unlike its antebellum precursor.

Republicans looked to courts in particular to move this project along because they were on the cusp of losing political power to the more localist Democrats in the House. Their continued grip on the Senate and the White House until 1885, meanwhile, ensured that they could staff the federal courts with sympathetic jurists. Using the courts as an instrument of their industrial policy had the added benefit of allowing the party to advance its economic nationalism agenda without having to place that set of policy priorities front and center in its election manifestos. A policy goal important to party supporters, but contentious among the wider public, could be pursued indirectly without becoming an electoral liability.[55] Federal judges tended to be sympathetic to the positions held by national corporate entities for reasons beyond the continued Republican grip on the appointments process. Unlike state court judges, federal judges did not have to stand for election. They were hence less influenced by public discontent about the growth of corporate power, and so less likely to support measures like the Granger Acts.

The Supreme Court also did its share to amplify the new jurisdictional grants. Its newly minted federal-question jurisdiction could not reach all cases in which national corporate interests were imperiled. In the 1885 Pacific Railroad Removal Case, though, the Court ruled that any suit against a federally chartered corporation, even if it implicated only ordinary state law claims and defenses, came within both the language of Article III and the removal provisions of the 1875 Act.[56] It's not clear that the Court understood the implication of that ruling for the lower courts. That decision, the future Supreme Court Justice Felix Frankfurter later noted, drove "an immense expansion in the business of the federal courts," perhaps unexpectedly. As this swelling caseload came into view, it nurtured a new concern about judges' dockets being "cluttered" with petty matters.[57]

Once created, moreover, federal court jurisdiction in this register proved hard to unravel. Legal scholars recently have stressed one reason: the difficulty that any national legislation faces in overcoming the many hurdles of committee review, bicameralism, and presentment to become law.[58] But that argument is at best incomplete. It does not distinguish proposals to change federal jurisdiction from any other federal bill. Likely more important was the fact that powerful lobbies, including railroads and other national companies, would have resisted any such repeal. Policies—including those entangled in the fashioning of federal courts—engender politics and new constituencies of their own accord. By successfully employing the federal courts to pursue their own policy goals in an unprecedented fashion, the Republicans also provided courts with a cushion of political support that made unlikely the sort of backsliding observed in 1802. Policy feedback, and not the mere fact of bicameralism, explains the political durability of jurisdiction.

Indeed, it is no surprise that Congress added to, rather than subtracted from, the courts as their jurisprudence of the national economy swelled. Most importantly, in 1891, the Evarts Act formed a new layer of intermediate appellate courts—yet another element of the 1801 Judiciary Act that had lain dormant, this one for almost a century.[59] A second set of institutional changes in the 1920s more subtly altered the standing of the federal courts vis-à-vis the other branches of the federal government. In 1922, the Judicial Conference Act, beyond creating new district judge positions, augmented the judiciary's power to manage itself. It allowed the Chief Justice to transfer district judges around to manage caseload problems. It also created a Conference of Senior Circuit Judges, headed by the Chief Justice, that would advise Congress on judicial reform.[60] In effect, the judiciary gained a bureaucratic armature with the Chief Justice at its apex.

Then the 1925 Judiciary Act—known as the Judges' Bill—changed the Supreme Court's role more still. Where once the Court had scant choice in which cases it heard, the Judges' Bill gave it discretion.[61] It could pick its cases. Choice meant that the Justices could not only selectively police the lower courts, but more importantly could shape the direction and pace of change in constitutional and federal law. The Court could decide, to a great extent, how to draw up the agenda for what legal and policy issues the judiciary would address, when, and how rapidly.[62] By endowing the Court with bureaucratic muscle, a seat at the negotiating table in Congress, and power to set the agenda of federal legal change, these acts dramatically altered the status of the judiciary as a *national political* body capable of organized, policy-focused action.

Strikingly, this last raft of measures was not the work of a political coalition pursuing a vision of national state-building and determined to yoke the federal courts into its service. Instead, it was the work of former president and then–Chief Justice William Howard Taft, who served as a principal drafter, main cheerleader, and also leading expert for Congress during the measures' enactment. The American Bar Association had also at this time become a powerful interest group supporting Taft's efforts. The ensuing bills, moreover, seemed "largely clerical" to many members of Congress, who perhaps did not fully appreciate the breadth of authority they were both ceding and seeding.[63] For the first time in American history, legislative reform of the judiciary was driven by an actor who spoke for the courts themselves, one who fortuitously also had experience and standing in the pell-mell of democratic politicking.

In roughly the half-century after the Civil War, the federal courts achieved a degree of autonomy and policy-making authority that would have been unthinkable in the early Republic. The causes of this transformation were a mix of tectonic movements in the national economy and the political genius of a single person. To be sure, it would be quite misleading to suggest that those courts were suddenly insulated against partisan pressures coming from Congress or the executive branch. Appointments would continue to be a powerful instrument for changing the Supreme Court in particular, as we shall see. And of course, Congress can simply change the substantive federal law or propose an amendment to the Constitution. In

1937, President Franklin Roosevelt's threat to bulk up the number of Justices on the Supreme Court absent retirements came in the wake of a series of decisions invalidating a first wave of New Deal statutes. Roosevelt's plan nearly came to fruition. In part, it was thwarted because of the Court's own savvy trimming of its sails through a series of decisions more favorable to federal power.[64]

But it is telling that Roosevelt made no public move to emulate President Jefferson in 1802, who had simply shown sixteen federal judges the door—good behavior be damned. So it was not just Maria, Paul, Jenny, Selah, Kate, and Anna who have been forgotten. The very idea that Congress could have plenary control over what federal courts exist, at least beyond the single Justice of the Supreme Court mandated by the Constitution, or that it is the absolute master of which jurisdictional springs will be tapped, has been lost. Perhaps the closest the New Deal debate came to this nation was the idea, floated in Congress, that by legislative directive the Court could be barred from invalidating legislation without a supermajority of seven.[65] If the true mark of power is not in making people obey, but in making them forget that they had the choice even to do otherwise, then the so-called court-packing crisis should be recognized for its revelations about the extent of, rather than the limits upon, judicial power. The very fact that Congress's near-plenary authority to control jurisdiction did not play a large role in that crisis shows how far the federal courts had come. What once was ordinary had become unthinkable.

Finally, the federal courts were free—or at least freer than they had ever been in the Republic's history. But free to do what?

CHAPTER 3

. . .

Remedies

It is damages or nothing.

Justice John Marshall Harlan II[1]

IT IS 1909. An African American woman named Lula Brawner is standing in her front yard in Elberton, Georgia, "attending to her domestic duties, at peace with all the world and demeaning herself as an orderly and law-abiding woman." Suddenly, the town's sheriff, W. H. Irwin, seizes her, places her under arrest, and then lights upon her with a whip. He is "cutting her flesh in scars, causing her much pain and suffering" while accusing her of having struck one of his relations. Brawner sues Irwin in federal court for damages. The district court turns away her plea, explaining that it has "no jurisdiction." The judge explains that it "does not appear from the declaration in this case that the defendant has deprived the plaintiff of any rights, privileges, or immunities secured by the Constitution and laws of the United States."[2] It is uncontested, though, that the sheriff, in arresting Lula, acted under a badge of state authority.

Fast-forward a century. It is 2010, and a fifteen-year-old, Sergio Adrián Hernández Güereca, is playing with friends in a cement culvert between El Paso, Texas, and Ciudad Juarez, Mexico. A Border Patrol agent, Jesus Mesa Jr., rides up on a bicycle and seizes one of Sergio's friends. Stones are thrown. Perhaps Sergio throws some of them. As Sergio runs away back to the Mexican side, unarmed and by all accounts unthreatening, Mesa shoots him twice. Sergio dies. A decade later, after long and a tortuous litigation process, Sergio's parents end up before the US Supreme Court in a pitched legal battle over whether they have even a right to sue Mesa for damages because of his unlawful, likely unconstitutional, killing of their son. They lose.[3] They are left bereft of kin and as empty-handed as Lula Brawner.

Separated by one hundred years, these cases are united by echoes as well as divided by differences. Start with the parallels. Both concern a state agent unleashing coercion in a devastating and likely unlawful way. In both instances, the victim of this violence was far from high and mighty. Both instead fell firmly within a socially marginal group. Both were already subject to a more extensive, and quite legal, regime of state violence. Such vulnerability is what it meant to be an African American living in the age of Jim Crow or to be a Mexican national living on the southern US border in an era of militarized border enforcement, mass deportations, and family separation. In neither case, however, did the plaintiff ask the federal courts to address those larger, structural forms of state violence. Neither case required the court to speak to the moral questions immanent in Jim Crow or the deportation state. Neither offered a lever for peeling back those state formations layer by layer in order to reach the core questions of political morality. Both plaintiffs framed instead narrower questions about discrete illegalities. In both cases, the courts turned a cold shoulder to the plaintiffs' carefully cabined pleas. In both cases, the victims ended with no redress and—importantly—state agents had emerged from the litigation with no legal reason to restrain their violence within the generous bounds of law.

Such strong parallels between 1909 and 2010 suggest that remedial collapse is not only a contemporary phenomenon. The similarities call for an explanation rooted in the blueprint of Article III and the courts' legacy of political influence and late-blooming institutional autonomy. This chapter and the next develop an account of why both Brawner and Hernández had no redress at law for unlawful state violence. This account is nested in the blueprint and historical construction of the federal courts recounted in Chapters 1 and 2. The account of constitutional remedies that follows stresses how the availability of constitutional remedies at a given moment has always been shaped by the Article III blueprint, subsequent partisan dynamics, and the resulting tides of American state-building. It is thus of a piece with the larger narrative of the judiciary's institutional development over time. Indeed, it cannot be understood apart from that story.

And yet the blueprint and construction of Article III courts do not inexorably lead to a remedial vacuum. In the middle of the twentieth century, the political dynamics that shaped the federal courts through the appointment process, and hence infused judges' perceptions of their own institutional prerogatives, led to some significant remediation of constitutional wrongs. Judges drew on statutes that had lain untouched since the Reconstruction period, refashioning procedural devices that had historically been deployed to protect national railroads from state regulation, while innovating to forge new remedies for criminal defendants and others exposed to state violence. The result was a renaissance of individual remedies for negative rights against state coercion from the 1950s to the early 1970s.

This blossoming, though, was short-lived. Partisan tides turned. Institutional imperatives soured. The federal court door closed once more. We can speak of collapse today because we have had a glimpse, however fleeting, of a better possibility.

THE DESPOTIC AMERICAN STATE STEPS UP

In a legal regime characterized by negative rights against the state and its coercive agents, but few positive rights to state aid, the importance of judicial remedies for constitutional violations depends in the first instance upon how and when the state can violate the Constitution. If the state is relatively modest in scope, with few instrumentalities for controlling its populations through coercion and surveillance, negative rights have relatively little role to play. Expand the state's forceful footprint, though, and these rights take on a new aspect. Whether the focus is on states and municipalities, or instead on the national government, the twentieth century has been marked by a tremendous growth in the American state's coercive capacity. An increase in the scope of state coercive apparatuses changes the stakes for constitutional remedies. So we should begin by asking: Against what kind of state do constitutional rights protect? Also, how have changes to that state affected the call for, and the ultimate effect of, judicial action over time?

At the turn of the twentieth century, the federal government's capacity for domestic coercion was relatively limited. In the useful formulation offered by sociologist Michael Mann, we can say that the pre-1900 American state had a good deal of "infrastructural power." By this term, Mann aimed the capacity to penetrate society and implement decisions through the coordinated actions of private actors—think here of the Fugitive Slave Acts as partially successful examples. But it lacked what Mann called "despotic power." This is the ability to coerce compliance directly.[4]

This deficiency was not to last. In 1909, when Lula Brawner was assaulted, the Federal Bureau of Investigation (FBI) was a fledging body merely a year old. By 2020, it employed some thirty-five thousand agents and support workers, sucking up an annual budget of some $9.3 billion. The bureau's growth was driven first by the 1919 Volstead Act. This launched Prohibition with a slate of new federal crimes and an attendant new swath of federal criminals.[5] Or consider immigration enforcement. In 1909, there was no Border Patrol. By 2020, that body had some 61,506 employees, including some 19,648 Border Patrol agents.[6] Other instrumentalities of coercion would emerge and grow in the postwar years. After World War II, the Central Intelligence Agency and National Security Agency emerged as instruments of security beyond the water's edge, but they would quickly come to be deployed closer to home against perceived domestic enemies. Programs such as COINTELPRO and its ilk grew through a process of subtle and insidious "mission creep."[7]

The twentieth century is often imagined as the era in which national military might extended overseas, creating for better or for worse a hegemonic postwar Pax Americana. But as important as this foreign deployment was the development of the internal capacity for coercion by the federal government—a development enabled by a wartime ballooning of federal power and resources in the 1940s. This in turn flowed from a new regime of mass income taxation and deficit spending.[8] Thanks to these new dollars, the infrastructural state could become something more despotic.

New implements of coercion created new opportunities for policy-making. These ranged from the moral crusade of the Volstead Act to the labor-market manipulation enabled by the deportation state. In turn, the popularity of these new coercive projects fostered public calls to Congress for more resources for a more fearsome despotic state. The ensuing drip feed of resources swelled the state's coercive muscles, and coercive agencies in time became an important and persistent interest group that could resist any backsliding in terms of financial or legislative support.

An example of this self-perpetuating dynamic is the immigration enforcement apparatus that ensnared Sergio Adrián Hernández Güereca. At the end of the nineteenth century, immigration law was enforced by a motley band of port-based customs officers whose main job was collecting taxes and enforcing passenger laws. Congress relied heavily on state officials rather than developing its own bureaucracy. Only in 1891 did Congress create a "superintendent of immigration" in the Treasury Department. But this new regulatory structure remained weak. By the turn of the twentieth century, only a few hundred people were being deported each year, despite the late-nineteenth-century push to oust Chinese and Japanese migrants from the West Coast. When Brawner's case was on the docket, deportations had risen to only a few thousand, while the number of migrants arriving was already in the six figures. It was in the 1930s, as the Great Depression crunched livelihoods, that President Franklin D. Roosevelt issued an executive order creating a new "Immigration and Naturalization Service" (INS) to regulate licit and illicit flows of bodies across borders. Congress piled on with new legal powers. Earlier, immigration agents had to creatively interpret federal statutes to lay claim to the authority to make arrests for violations of immigration laws. But Congress in 1946 formally gave them power to make warrantless arrests of any noncitizen violating the immigration laws who was "likely to escape before a warrant" could be secured.

The history of immigration enforcement also suggests how the development of coercive state instrumentalities can take on a life of its own. As those instruments are built up, their institutional leaders seize upon ambiguities in the relevant legislative authorization to assert a broad mandate, such as the power to make arrests. Once constructed, coercive agencies such as the INS also become fixtures in Congress, capable of defending and enlarging their prerogatives through the lobbying process.[9] Elected politicians also look to coercive federal agencies to solve unanticipated problems and crises that fall outside the parameters of civilian agencies, from the Mariel Boatlift of 1980 to the attacks of September 11, 2001. New crises translate into new opportunities to showcase agencies' importance, which in turn amplify the agencies' political clout and prestige for later battles over governmental resources.

A similar story can be told about the local policing bodies that figure in *Brawner*. Policing in the United States has long been a decentralized affair. Broadly stated, it is supplied by municipalities and counties, although states play important roles in funding and regulating the resulting bodies under arms. At the time of the nation's founding, cities tended to have loosely organized night watches or constabularies managed by judges. Following the model of London's metropolitan force, the first municipal police force was established in Boston in 1838. New York City followed suit in 1845, Philadelphia in 1855, and Baltimore in 1857. The less urbanized South pursued a different path. Antebellum "slave patrols" evolved into paramilitary groups during the Jim Crow era. These were tasked with keeping African Americans in a subordinate social and economic rank.[10] In both North and South, the institution of police grew in terms of sheer numbers and powers throughout the twentieth century. The mass production of the automobile led to the growth of traffic policing and the emergence of state-level police forces to shore up the work of their urban counterparts.[11] Today, there are more than eighteen thousand police jurisdictions in the United States, employing some nine hundred thousand armed officers and four hundred thousand civilians.[12] These state and local forces are an order of magnitude more numerous than federal coercive agencies. They are also a far more immediate presence in most people's lives.

As with federal law enforcement, an important element of the growth in policing power has been the emergence of new legal authorities and their promiscuous redeployment by creative officials. A good example is a police officer's authority to stop a person on the street without a warrant on the suspicion that the person is involved in some kind of criminality. This was rarely spelled out by ordinance or rule. It has taken on a life of its own, thanks to judicial rulings.

The Supreme Court first addressed the question whether this power complied with the Constitution's Fourth Amendment in the 1960 case of *Terry v. Ohio*. The *Terry* Court, in a carefully worded and narrowly drawn decision, held that an officer is entitled to make a "brief" nonconsensual "investigatory stop" if he or she has "reasonable articulable suspicion" that a crime either has occurred or is about to occur.[13] In *Terry* itself, the officer had observed armed suspects casing a store with an apparent eye to its potentially violent robbery. That is, the case itself framed the power to make stops in terms of a serious, potentially violent, crime.

Once unleashed, though, the *Terry* power proved impossible to limit. Stops are a highly discretionary decision. They are dispersed in space and time. They are also hard to supervise even within the police force. The vague and open-ended *Terry* standard invited police action well beyond those instances in which a serious and imminent crime was in the offing. By the end of the twentieth century, the *Terry* stop had experienced metastatic growth. In New York, there were 313,047 documented stops in 2004, 576,394 stops in 2009, and 685,724 stops in 2011. Between 2004 and 2013, that city's inhabitants experienced roughly 5 million street stops. Statistics from other cities, including Chicago, Baltimore, and Philadelphia, tell a similar tale.[14] At the same time, it would be a mistake to think that this was the whole story, or that police have been single-mindedly focused on crime control. Even in the early decades of the twentieth century, police experienced a more substantive mission creep. They took in tramps, returned lost children by the thousands, shot stray dogs, enforced sanitation laws, inspected boilers, took annual censuses, and on occasion broke strikes.[15] The present tendency to use the police as a general-purpose solution to all social ills—a tendency that only feeds the growth of the coercive state—thus has deep roots.

The federal deportation state and America's policing state both grew partly because they came to be closely entangled with majoritarian anxieties about race and ethnicity. The connection between racial anxiety and the nation's immigration infrastructure goes back to the very first federal immigration measures targeting Chinese migrants in the 1870s and 1880s. Large racial disparities in policing and incarceration appeared first during the Great Migration of the early twentieth century, when African Americans moved en masse to northern industrial centers and became subjects of race-conscious social control by urban police forces.[16] The racial cast of the punitive state is an old one. Even today, the size of a local jurisdiction's police force remains tightly correlated with its racial and ethnic composition even after controlling for crime rates. Moreover, while spending on police tends to rise as a locality becomes more racially and ethnically diverse, spending on other public goods, such as roads and sanitation, tends to fall.[17] The story of the despotic state at both the national and the local level, therefore, cannot be untangled from the twentieth-century struggle over White supremacy in America.

INDIVIDUALIZED JUDICIAL REMEDIES AND THE DESPOTIC STATE

Equally, the idea of federal courts as a source for constitutional remedies cannot be decoupled from these histories of American state development. Yet the relationship between the federal courts and the twentieth-century rise of the coercive state has several strands that need to be untangled.

To begin with, courts have always had an ambiguous relationship with state power. A court's intervention can either be generative or constraining for the state. On the one hand, the growth in despotic power at plural levels of government was the sine qua non of the revolution in individual remedies. It furnished occasions for the display of judicial authority. Yet the *Terry* decision is a reminder of the possibility that federal courts can inadvertently *create* pathways for institutional innovation and expansion. Indeed, they can do so even as they are being called upon to provide a remedy to an individual litigant, and even if they think they are describing a tightly cabined state authority. *Terry* is not unique. There are many decisions in the policing and immigration arenas in which courts have ratified or invited innovative uses of coercive powers.

Terry is a nice illustration, indeed, of how the judicial power to craft new, generally applicable law is entangled with the courts' power to remedy individual wrongs. Nothing about this intertwining is inevitable. The power to remedy might be completely detached from the power to declare new interpretations of the Constitution. Indeed, in respect to many kinds of individual remedies, the Supreme Court has stipulated that only those rights holders who can show that their claim requires the fashioning of nothing new so far as law goes can receive a remedy. This decouples the remedial function from the law-declaration function.

Further, the practical effect of individualized judicial remedies on absolute levels of state coercion can change quite dramatically as the coercive state grows in scale. Calls for court-imposed constraints, on the one hand, are likely to grow louder as the size of the state's various coercive institutions expand, at whatever level of government. The more border agents there are, the greater the likelihood that a stray bullet will hit another Sergio Hernández. At the same time, in the mine-run of cases, a discrete action for damages or some other form of individualized relief is rarely going to challenge directly the underlying metastatic growth of the coercive state. These actions attack only the small fraction of illicit state coercion, whether by the police or the Border Patrol. Most unlawful violence is never challenged in court: Much even goes invisible and unpunished. Moreover, when state agents are allowed wide discretion to use force by law, remedies for unlawful action will do little to constrain the absolute quantum of state violence for the simple reason that much of that violence will be lawful (and it may well be hard to distinguish in practice the lawful from the illicit). An expansion of the coercive state hence increases the demand for judicial interventions to correct lawless violence, but at the same time diminishes the marginal effect of such remedies on the average person's exposure to state coercion. As there is more lawful coercion, in other words, the regulation of discrete incidents of unlawful coercion becomes less significant as a practical matter from the citizen's perspective.

How the availability of individual remedies inflects the public's view of lawful coercive power is also ambiguous. It may be that the seeing courts remedying state violence flags for the public the downside of coercive institutions, and that this induces more resistance to the expansion of violent state capacities. Or it might be that judicial intervention is perceived as resolving the moral difficulty of an amped-up coercive state. This would result in more public quietism and acceptance of state violence. How these cross-cutting legitimation effects play out in practice is difficult to predict, and probably varies from moment to moment.

Despite these complexities, there are still powerful justifications for courts being in the business of providing individualized remedies. Had Brawner or the Hernández family received the damages they had sought, the ensuing awards would have furthered the moral end of correcting a wrong inflicted by a state agent. What legal philosophers call "corrective justice" would thus have been vindicated.[18] There is much to be said for the thought that the Hernández family deserved not just a day in court but some legally sanctioned recognition of their wrongful loss. Perhaps this is enough to justify remedies' price tag.

Moreover, beyond the experience of a particular victim, a public whose dearly held interest in life or liberty can be extinguished without consequence is a public that likely experiences a certain demoralization as a consequence of the pervasive anticipation of unchecked state violence. Or, perhaps more precisely, if you are socially marginal and politically powerless, your natural state will be fear and anxiety about unregulated state violence. (The wealthy and the powerful, of course, generally have ways to shield themselves from the state's depredations). From the vantage of the lone citizen, the idea that she is without recourse after being seriously harmed by the state cannot be a happy one. More likely, it will seep into and taint her encounters with state officials. The absence of any remedy is also a legal correlate of the more general idea that the law simply does not apply to those wielding the state's cudgel. Such a state of affairs offends an elemental tenet of the rule of law: the idea, as the legal philosopher Joseph Raz puts it, that "people in government, just like anybody else, should obey the law."[19] A legal system without remedies for the wrongs of powerful officials is, definitionally, missing the rule of law. These nonconsequentialist grounds for constitutional remedies likely do enough justificatory work for many people.

On the forward-facing side of the ledger, there are reasons for thinking that state agencies will not necessarily change their behavior as a result of a single damages award. Politicians, after all, chase votes, not dollars. Governments may also be so large that even a stream of damages judgments does not dent their overall fiscal picture. For example, my city of Chicago paid out $100 million in settlements and damages due to police brutality in 2018 alone, yet took few effectual steps to quell such violence in subsequent years; quite the contrary, three years later, the police department had experienced very little reform despite the Black Lives Matter movement.[20] Nationally, the seemingly endless drumbeat of disproportionately African American and men and women shot, suffocated, choked, and beaten to death by police across the nation suggests that the notional availability of a damages remedy is no cure-all.

Still, it would be a mistake to think that the insufficiency of judicial remedies as a panacea for government overreach saps them of *any* forward-facing justification. There's reason to think instead that remedies have some welcome incentive effects. Many cities and counties with police forces, for example, take out liability insurance to cover anticipated damages awards. Even if this renders government entities somewhat indifferent to their own constitutional wrongs, the insurance firms covering those losses do have a fiscal interest in controlling the number of damages suits. They intervene in police training and regulation to promote less violent forms of policing.[21] Lawsuits can act also as sources of information in dispersed state bureaucracies. A police chief in a large city or county might use them to learn which of his officers have a propensity for excessive force. In the absence of liability, victims may not have an incentive to come forward with information about problematic officers—especially if they fear that doing so will expose them to further risks of official violence. In addition, the prospect of a trial and personal liability can have reputational effects for individual officials. Being publicly accused of improper actions is an embarrassment, even if your legal fees and ultimate liabilities are likely covered by your employer. Finally, constitutional remedies can take forms other than cash payments. Some are potentially more effective at stimulating changes in state behaviors.

The effect of judicial remedies on the sheer frequency of constitutional violations, therefore, turns on the perspective one takes. If the aim is wholesale reform of the violent American state, then individualized remedies are unlikely to be useful. Negative rights against the state do little to correct deep economic and social inequalities: They are necessarily shallow in reach. Further, the right against unlawful state violence matters only to the extent that a democratic government doesn't license such violence by law. Despite this, remedies can be warranted for corrective justice, rule-of-law protection, democratic ethics, and even consequentialist reasons. The question that follows is whether the courts will provide them.

THE RISE OF REMEDIES

The seeds for a comprehensive regime of constitutional remedies were laid by statute in the Civil War's wake. As we saw in Chapter 2, the Radical Republican Congress of the 1860s passed a series of measures to expand access to the federal courts—understood at the time as an instrument of a federal policy for reconstructing the former Confederate states. Yet as the national commitment to Reconstruction sputtered and died, so too did the political and the judicial will to defend the individual rights of Black freedmen and their allies. Statutes enacted for that end were left as lonely relics, marooned without apparent purpose on the statute books. Two, in particular, would fall into desuetude only to spring back to life in the middle of the twentieth century.

The first important Reconstruction-era statute was enacted in response to postwar violence targeting former slaves. A mix of criminal prohibitions and civil actions, the 1871 Ku Klux Klan Act allowed for money-damages actions against state, but not federal, officials alleged to have violated the Constitution. Its key provision is now widely known as "Section 1983" after the place in the statute books where it can be found. Section 1983 allows a person to sue an official for damages if the defendant was acting "under color" of state (not federal) law.[22] Sheriff Irwin should have been a plausible defendant because he was acting under state law when he arrested and then whipped Lula. But the Border Patrol agent Mesa would have been beyond the statute's ken because the federal government paid his salary. Section 1983 was, however, rarely used in the late nineteenth and early twentieth centuries. One survey of its first sixty-five years found only nineteen reported decisions, including Lula Brawner's.[23]

The *Brawner* case provides an insight into why Section 1983 was so little used. Federal judges initially read the Constitution's limitations on state actors exceedingly narrowly. They also held that the Bill of Rights located in the Constitution's first nine amendments simply did not extend to the several states. New constitutional rights created by the 1868 Fourteenth Amendment were hence stingily doled out.[24] At the same time, courts also took a pinched view of what counted as "under color" of law—as Brawner's case once again illustrated. In an era when private and public violence often intermingled for the purpose of maintaining formal and informal racial hierarchy, the judicial effort to draw a distinction between them was an invitation to circumvent federal law's protections.

The second important Reconstruction-era measure was an amendment to the 1789 Judiciary Act. This 1867 measure expanded the federal courts' power to issue "the writ of habeas corpus."[25] Enacted little more than a year after the Thirteenth Amendment's prohibition on slavery came into force, the 1867 law reached "any person restrained of his or her liberty." Its sponsor in the House, Representative William Lawrence, described it as a "bill of the largest liberty."[26] His aspiration had some historical pedigree. An invention of English law, the habeas writ began as a mechanism for the monarchy's highest courts to supervise the activities of vassal jurisdictions by requiring them to furnish an explanation whenever they detained a person. Liberty could only be taken away in compliance with the king's wishes. In the course of early-seventeenth-century confrontations between the king and Parliament, however, the habeas writ became a more flexible instrument that did not merely serve the royal will. It was used by English courts to test the legality of detention in the hands of any executive official, including the Crown's men. As such, it inspired the Constitution's drafters to include language in the Constitution limiting Congress's "suspension" of the writ's availability.

The Suspension Clause, as it has come to be known, in its turn prompted the inclusion of a grant of habeas jurisdiction in the Judiciary Act of 1789. This eighteenth-century provision, though, was never intended to apply to detention in the hands of a state official. It only covered detention by federal actors. The 1867 habeas statute broke new ground by allowing any person detained by a state official to seek federal court review. Like Section 1983, at first the new habeas power was not extensively used to police the burgeoning state criminal justice systems of the Gilded Age or Progressive Era. Instead, it too lay "a sleeping giant" for decades, on the books but rarely invoked as a basis for federal court action.[27]

In the 1950s the Supreme Court revived these two moribund statutes, part of a larger revolution in individual remedies. Beyond resuscitating Section 1983 and habeas, the Court in *Mapp v. Ohio* fashioned an "exclusion" remedy for police searches in violation of the Fourth Amendment's protection against unreasonable searches and seizures. Next, acknowledging that Section 1983 extended to state but not federal actors, the Court crafted a new vehicle for damages against individual federal officials who used unconstitutional violence. At roughly the same time, the Justices were also extending more provisions of the Bill of Rights to the states. This complicated the lattice of constitutional rules and remedies covering police investigations and the criminal trial process. The Court undertook this enterprise in light of its growing understanding of how criminal justice institutions worked as bulwarks for Jim Crow.[28]

What ensued from the 1950s and 1960s was not just a thicker conception of constitutional rights against state violence, more closely adapted to the policing state that had emerged in the early twentieth century. This period also yielded an arsenal of judicial devices that victims of unlawful state coercion could deploy to obtain some compensation or other remedy. To be sure, in all but a few cases, this judicial response would be focused and limited to a single rights holder. Courts offered no global solutions to the secular increase in state violence, but only individualized balm. But for the Lula Brawners of the world, who had labored under the whip of a repressive state apparatus for decades, even that little hope and small gain must have seemed sweet indeed.

Four Supreme Court decisions worked to burst the remedial dam and refashion federal courts into meaningful guardians of individual constitutional rights. These marquee cases of the individual remedies revolution must be understood, though, in light of other elements of federal law that enabled systemic challenges to state policies. Let us consider each in turn, and then place them in a wider context.

Perhaps the most important case came from the Court in 1961. Like many northern cities, Chicago had been transformed by the Great Migration. Between 1940 and 1960, the city's Black population grew by a half million, spilling out from the southern Black belt into new neighborhoods across the city. To say the least, this was not to the liking of many White residents of the Windy City. Through the first half of the twentieth century, violent race riots flared. In this fraught context, a White insurance agent, Peter Saisi, was shot in his home office one evening. At the time, his family was upstairs. His wife, Mary, a "demure, 120-pound brunette," spun a tale of "two Negros" entering the Saisi home and confronting her husband. On the basis of Mary's—false—testimony and speedy identification of a face in a lineup, Chicago detective Frank Pape raced to the Garfield Park home of James Monroe, without waiting for an arrest warrant, to grab and lock up the father of six. Pape literally dragged Monroe from his bed, while his wife and children were held at gunpoint. One officer saw fit to give one of the Monroe children, a four-year-old, an educative kicking in the process. Pilloried with racial epithets, Monroe was shackled and dragged out of doors. His home meanwhile was ransacked for evidence that was not there.

The next day, Mary was brought to the station. She was unable to pick out James Monroe in a lineup. He was released and, with the aid of a lawyer from the local American Civil Liberties Union affiliate, filed suit for damages against Pape and the other officers. Later, Mary's lover confessed to the crime—sending the pair of them to prison for decades.[29]

As in the *Brawner* case, the district court and the court of appeals declined to extend Monroe any remedy. His relief, they said, had to come from a state court under state law. But the Supreme Court accepted Monroe's request for a hearing and reversed the lower courts' rulings. Justice William O. Douglas's opinion for eight Justices expended most of its energy discussing the text of the statute to show that Pape could be sued in federal court even though his actions had been unlawful under state law. Leaning into the historical context of the Ku Klux Klan Act, Douglas explained that the 1871 Act had been "passed to afford a federal right in federal courts because, by reason of prejudice, passion, neglect, intolerance or otherwise, state laws might not be enforced and the claims of citizens to the enjoyment of rights, privileges and immunities guaranteed by the Fourteenth Amendment might be denied by the state agencies."[30]

Monroe had an electric effect. Between 1961 and 1988, the number of civil rights suits filed under Section 1983 (excluding prisoners' suits) leaped from 150 to 42,354.[31] Seventeen years after *Monroe*, the Court extended the range of actors who could be sued for damages. In *Monell v. Department of Social Services*, the Court allowed civil rights plaintiffs to haul deep-pocketed municipalities into federal court too.[32] The exposure of cities to suits also allowed civil rights plaintiffs to challenge not just discrete acts but policies for which the city was responsible, such as flawed training or hiring protocols. Since many constitutional rights violations are best addressed through programmatic change anyway, *Monell* opened one of the few pathways to meaningful institutional reform through the courts.

The ability to sue officers and municipalities for money damages mattered, and still matters, a great deal as it is not possible to sue the state directly because of a doctrine called "sovereign immunity." This means simply that a private party cannot haul either a state government or the federal government into federal or state court. In a line of cases dating back to 1890, the Supreme Court has interpreted the Eleventh Amendment to the Constitution to embody this general principle of sovereign immunity.[33] The language of the Eleventh Amendment itself picks out only cases "commenced or prosecuted against one of the United States by Citizens of another State, or by Citizens or Subjects of any Foreign State." It only addresses federal courts and, even then, is focused on a limited set of cases. On the Court's reading, though, the Eleventh Amendment's text is less relevant than an alleged background legal principle of sovereign immunity. Ignoring the Constitution's text, as well as considerable evidence from the early Republic, the Court has brocaded together different elements of eighteenth-century international law, common law, and English practice into a legal rule to the effect that states can almost never be sued without their consent by a private party in federal court, their own courts, another state's courts, or even before a federal administrative agency. Sovereign immunity means that "officer suits" under Section 1983—for example, ones that name a specific individual officer as a defendant—are often the sole mechanism for extracting compensation for state violence.

The second important case of the individual remedies revolution, *Brown v. Allen*, was initially three different cases arising from North Carolina state courts in the early 1950s. They were consolidated before the Supreme Court because all raised questions about the scope of the 1867 habeas statute. Clyde Brown was an illiterate Black youth from Winston-Salem, North Carolina. He was arrested for the beating and rape of a White high school student. He was then held without charges for five days, without access to a lawyer or to his family. During these five days incommunicado, he made a confession. Another thirteen days later, he was brought before a judge for a preliminary hearing; three days after that, he got a lawyer. In the second case, Raleigh Speller was described in court papers as "an illiterate and feeble-minded Negro of about forty-six years of age." He was convicted of the rape of a fifty-two-year-old White housewife and sentenced to death. In a third case, two cousins, Lloyd Ray Daniels and Bennie Daniels—again illiterate, Black teenagers— were arrested before dawn on a February morning and imprisoned on suspicion of the murder of a White taxicab driver. Both were convicted and sentenced to death.

In each of these three cases, the defendants challenged their final state court convictions by filing a habeas action in the North Carolina federal courts, citing the 1867 statute as a basis for jurisdiction. In each of these new postconviction federal court actions, the Black criminal defendant raised constitutional concerns about the investigations and the criminal adjudications that had resulted in their sentences. Each claimed that the jury selection process for their trials had been tainted by racial bias. Brown also claimed police had beaten his confession out of him. All were turned aside by the federal lower courts, despite the seeming breadth of the 1867 statute, without any ruling on the cases' merits.[34]

When these cases arrived at the Supreme Court, it was apparent that the Justices had already started to wrestle more seriously with questions of jurisdiction and the nature of review that the 1867 statute might allow. Initially argued in 1952, the *Brown* cases at first confounded the Court. Justice Felix Frankfurter circulated a note to his colleagues saying, "I give up!"—a sentiment that might have been more mirthful had not a bevy of capital sentences been on the table. The three cases were held over to be reargued the following year. By coincidence, the following year, yet another matter denominated *Brown* would be held over for reargument by the Justices, and then resolved to rather more famous effect. The convergence in timing of cases challenging criminal justice and segregated schools as elements of Jim Crow, of course, was no happenstance.

The result that the *Brown v. Allen* Court ultimately settled on was less than clear. A flurry of opinions ensued, with the Justices plainly divided against each other. Oddly, Justice Stanley Reed's principal opinion has proved less influential than a separate writing by Justice Frankfurter, which was styled as a joint expression of "[t]he views of the Court on these questions." Frankfurter sketched a rather elaborate, six-step approach to the different types of factual and legal questions presented in habeas cases. In a particularly important procedural holding, he directed that a final resolution of an issue by the state courts, even with review by the US Supreme Court, did not prevent later habeas review—as some had previously believed. *Brown*'s bottom line, by a 6–3 margin, had to be pieced together from seven different opinions. It was that none of the defendants were entitled to any relief—but that habeas might be a remedy in later cases for someone else. This satisfied few. Among the broader public, the *Brown v. Allen* opinions were criticized as contradictory and incoherent. "There may be a 'rule of law' in those cases but the lawyers are going to be busy as little moles digging it out," complained the *Wall Street Journal*. "It left us confused."[35] Yet *Brown v. Allen* was to have a tremendous effect upon rates of postconviction challenges to state criminal convictions. Volumes of postconviction filings in federal courts rose precipitously in its wake—even as levels of school segregation remained constant after *Brown v. Board of Education*.

The third important case of midcentury had no Reconstruction-era foundation. The Fourth Amendment's protection against unreasonable searches and seizures is most often implicated when the police are investigating a crime. Where inculpating evidence is found, police will likely hand it over to prosecutors for use in a subsequent criminal trial. Since 1914, a criminal defendant in a federal criminal court could ask a judge to set aside—or "exclude"—evidence secured by unconstitutional means.[36] In 1949, the Supreme Court held that the Fourth Amendment bound state as well as federal officials.[37] This reversed a position held by the Court since the 1830s that the Bill of Rights did not bind the states. But in practice, the 1949 decision had very little effect because the Court declined to mandate the exclusion of unconstitutionally gained evidence. Damages actions are usually irrelevant to a criminal defendant facing prison, so state police had no real incentive to change their behavior after 1949. Not until 1961 did the Court change tack on remedies.[38]

Four years earlier, an African American woman, Dollree Mapp, had been living with her daughter in Cleveland, Ohio. Mapp's ex-husband had underworld ties. Her home came under suspicion after the home of Don King, a numbers racketeer and later boxing promoter, was bombed. When police arrived at Mapp's house, she refused them entry without a warrant. Rather than a warrant, police fetched backup. Fifteen men broke into Mapp's home, waving a paper they claimed was a warrant. Mapp grabbed it, stuffing it down her blouse. An officer yanked it out again. Mapp never got to see the paper. She was later arraigned on charges of having obscene material—a pile of novels, including one called *Affairs of a Troubadour*—in her home.[39] Reviewing her motion to exclude that evidence, the Supreme Court reversed course on Fourth Amendment remedies, and required exclusion of the evidence against Dollree Mapp. The result of the *Mapp* decision was that police officers, while unlikely to face money damages, had a professional incentive to follow constitutional rules. If they didn't, their cleared cases could be derailed by exclusionary motions keeping out the evidence that they had acquired.

Finally, federal officials had to fight habeas filings and exclusion motions. But they lacked any exposure to financial loss related to constitutional wrongs because Section 1983 applied only to state officials. This changed in 1965 when six FBI agents burst into Webster Bivens's Brooklyn home, seized and manacled him, and dragged him away for booking and interrogation. No charges resulted. Like Alexander Baxter, Bivens filed his own pro se lawsuit seeking damages. A major hurdle to his suit, ironically, was Section 1983. This provision made it abundantly clear that Congress had authorized suits against state officials for constitutional wrongs, but at the time Congress had enacted no explicit parallel authorization to sue federal officials for constitutional wrongs. One plausible inference to draw from this contrast of legislative action and silence was that suits for federal officials' constitutional wrongs were not permitted. His suit turned aside by the lower courts, Bivens won a surprising victory in the Supreme Court in 1971. As the concurring Justice John Harlan observed, "For people in Bivens' shoes, it is damages or nothing."[40] Rather than nothing, the Court held that "people in Bivens' shoes" had a right to file suit in federal court—called a "right of action" after an ancient procedural quiddity of the English legal system— notwithstanding the absence of any federal legislative analog to Section 1983.

These were far from the only important legal developments in the mid-twentieth century. To the contrary, this was a moment of substantial change in the federal court's public role—often with unexpected political effects. In the criminal justice domain, the Supreme Court experimented with prophylactic rules to mitigate the incidence of constitutional violations in the first instance. In 1966, for example, it imposed the famous *Miranda* warnings as a way of protecting criminal suspects from coercive interrogation.[41] As candidate for president, Richard Nixon would take aim at *Miranda*, as well as other criminal justice rules, in campaign speeches and in a position paper titled "Freedom from Fear."[42] Meanwhile, in a series of school desegregation cases that crescendoed simultaneously with *Brown v. Allen*, the federal courts developed a set of injunctive tools, including pupil assignment plans and busing, in their efforts to disembed racial segregation from schools. It is a nice and telling irony that the structural injunction deployed against Jim Crow schools in these desegregation cases evolved out of a procedural device first refined by the federal courts in the late 1800s as a means of shielding railroad companies from unconstitutional state rate-making.[43] Judicial solicitude for national corporations had provoked popular ire. Similarly, injunctions' use in the desegregation context, particularly to order the busing of children to achieve integration, provoked sharp public discontent. This fed, over time, into an important, conservative shift in suburban voters' political preferences.[44] The liberal Court of the 1950s and 1960s in this way was to prove its own gravedigger.

The midcentury revolution in individualized remedies hence did not happen in isolation. Rather, it was part of a broader, more complex shift in the working of the federal courts and federal adjudication across the board.

ENGINES OF THE INDIVIDUAL REMEDIES REVOLUTION

The emergence of a robust, four-pillared regime of individual remedies cries out for explanation. It is especially striking that none of the major remedial shifts of this era were accomplished through legislation. (The Administrative Procedures Act, enacted in June 1946, was an important federal statute that provided for remedies against federal agencies and that was a result of Congress's labor. The APA, as it is known, is not primarily concerned with constitutional violations, and so does not fit well in this survey). All four wellsprings of the remedial revolution emphasized here were the work of the courts, even if legislation lurked somewhere in the background. But why did the Court revive Section 1983 and the 1867 habeas statute? And why did it supplement those remedies with the exclusionary rule and the *Bivens* remedy—both instruments lacking any statutory foundation?

The liberalization of individual rights is best understood as a result of the same partisan forces that have shaped the judiciary by dint of the Article III blueprint and its frailties since the late eighteenth century. In the mid-twentieth century, however, the political forces shaping the courts favored a measure of racial remediation. This liberalization of remedies also reflected a changing set of institutional priorities on the judiciary's part— one that embodied a broad effort to establish their legitimacy as a major actor on the national stage. The Court would increasingly defend its authority by invoking its role vindicating individual rights. This change in legitimation strategies could be expressed thanks to the Court's institutional autonomy, itself a result of the Taft reforms of the 1920s. The midcentury was a moment, in other words, in which external political forces and the judiciary's own incentives converged to yield some benefits for individual rights holders previously excluded from political and legal concern.

For starters, that James Monroe, Dollree Mapp, Clyde Brown and codefendants, and Webster Bivens were all Black was no coincidence. At a time of widespread Black disenfranchisement, particularly in the South, it should be puzzling that the African American litigant prevailed in three of these four cases, if not in *Brown v. Allen*. It should be even more surprising that their victories and defeats alike would be generative in ways that could chaff against the growing despotic power of the American state. These cases, however, must be understood in terms of the Court's more general tilt against Jim Crow. This turn against American apartheid entailed a reconsideration of remedies because of the way that—in rural North Carolina and northern cities such as Chicago and Cleveland alike—policing and criminal justice institutions played a crucial role in expressing and preserving racial hierarchies.

Change once again started at the appointment stage. A fresh crop of judicial nominations under President Franklin D. Roosevelt created a liberal bench willing to take on Jim Crow institutions. Stymied from extending the benefits of New Deal programs beyond largely White populations by the resistance of southern Democratic politicians, Roosevelt looked to the federal courts as an instrument of racial change outside of legislative channels. He hoped racially liberal judges could help open the door to greater political participation by disenfranchised minorities, which would loosen the tight grip of southern Democrats on the national legislative agenda and also on his own party. Among his Supreme Court appointments, for example, was former attorney general Frank Murphy, an unjustly forgotten jurist who created a Civil Rights Section within the Department of Justice to push litigation to defend the political rights of citizens, particularly African

Americans. Under Roosevelt, the Justice Department also established a practice of intervention in civil rights cases in the federal courts. Among its targets was the so-called White primary, used in the South to lock in segregationist control of the Democratic ticket.[45] Federal lawyers also supported litigation challenges to racially restrictive covenants that were instrumental in creating residential segregation.[46] As in the 1870s, federal court appointments became a vehicle for successfully pursuing a policy goal that would have electorally strained the president's party.

A second reason that elected actors turned to the judiciary to change policy was geopolitical in character. As the historian Mary Dudziak has documented, an important pressure upon the national government, nudging it toward supporting racial reform, came from the imperatives of Cold War competition. As Secretary of State Dean Acheson put it, Jim Crow and its accoutrements were "a source of constant embarrassment to this Government in the day-to-day conduct of its foreign relations; [Jim Crow] jeopardize[d] the effective maintenance of our moral leadership of the free and democratic nations of the world."[47] Dudziak has powerfully documented links between Acheson's geostrategic worry and the school desegregation cases. Other historians have noted the ways in which the picture of violent, race-related repression more generally was "internationally delegitimating."[48] A wealth of historical evidence hence shows direct linkages between Cold War concerns and desegregation, but not necessarily the individual remedies cases. Yet the two lines of cases--concerning remedies and equality in secondary schooling— are hard to untangle from each other in terms of moral orientation. Once federal judges had been sensitized to these Cold War concerns respecting race relations, it is difficult to see why this concern would be limited to school- and housing-related cases. Indeed, at least once, the Supreme Court pointedly defined appropriate American policing in contrast to authoritarian Soviet practices.[49] So again, the public policy concerns of elected-branch actors shared across party lines are plausibly understood as driving changes to remedial doctrines.

These dynamics, despite their divergent partisan and geostrategic origins, aligned with a more general vector of American statebuilding during the twentieth century. Of the four critical cases imposing new individual remedies, three entailed state actors, and only one federal agents. Hence, these cases largely involved a federal body imposing remedial regimes upon local institutions for distinctively national policy ends. As such, these cases involved the exercise of federal authority by the courts to achieve national ends at the expense of states' and localities' autonomy. All this is consistent with the larger arc of twentieth-century state development in which the federal government gained greater effectual policy-making power at a quicker pace than its state analogs.

At the same time, the constraining effect of these decisions on state power should not be overstated. Federal courts checked at the margin the excesses of state actors, and in the case of *Bivens* remedies, the growing federal law enforcement apparatus. This national regime did not necessarily place an absolute limit on the size of the local coercive state. States, after all, remained free to expand their criminal justice budgets or to enlarge the domain of conduct subject to criminal penalties. And indeed, many did. Across the nation, police spending rose on average $4,760 per 1,000 inhabitants between 1980 and 2010.[50] Rather than capping the coercive state, the Court's remedial elaborations accompanied its steady inflation. They fashioned an increasingly national body of rules that aimed, however imperfectly, to regularize the discretionary use of state coercion—and so perhaps legitimated it somewhat in the eyes of the public. *Mapp* and *Brown v. Allen*, hence, involved extensions of rules for federal actors to state actors, while *Monroe* and *Bivens* can be understood as imposing functionally parallel checks on state and federal actors. The effect of judicial intervention is thus more accurately described as standardization—binding together the nation in a uniform regulatory regime—rather than limitation.

At the same time, the Court as an institution benefited from its forays into constitutional remedies. The project of addressing errant state violence against individual members of minority groups became a potent element of the courts' legitimizing strategy in this period. In Laura Kalman's authoritative account of legal culture in the 1960s, "legal liberalism" provided a legitimating justification for legal institutions. Legal liberalism reposed faith in the courts, and in particular the Supreme Court, to pursue inclusive social reforms for marginalized social groups, including African Americans, women, and workers.[51] Individual rights cases such as *Mapp*, *Monroe*, and *Bivens* fell squarely within this ideological matrix. By taking the lead in the national project of racial reform, particularly of criminal justice institutions, federal courts affirmed their own centrality in the legal liberalism framework. Law schools, the legal academy, and lawyers could bask in the reflected glory of the federal courts. Their admiration and praise, in return, invested the Court with a potential source of public support and legitimation. To be sure, few judges would consciously ask themselves what the faculty of an elite law school would have thought about an individual remedies case. Certainly, that thought could never be uttered out loud. But it is plausible to think that the ambient tug of social and professional networks that broadly approved of the Court's remedial interventions provided a powerful force, grounded in judges' self-interest, driving these results.

But faith in the courts as liberal engines of social change would not endure. Growing public discontent at the costs of desegregation, as well as swelling public concern over rising crime rates, would soon press the elected branches, and thence the courts, toward a very different posture toward remedies. Collapse was, in short, on the horizon, even at the moment of triumph.

CHAPTER 4

. . .

Collapse

Where a specific duty is assigned by law, and individual rights depend upon the performance of that duty, it seems equally clear that the individual who considers himself injured, has a right to resort to the laws of his country for a remedy.

Chief Justice John Marshall[1]

So WHAT WOULD happen to Lula Brawner today?

It is a warm May evening in Tucson, Arizona. It is 2010, the year of the death of Sergio Adrián Hernández Güereca. Amy Hughes is standing in her yard. She is trying to trim one of her trees with a knife and talking amicably to her housemate, Sharon Chadwick. No one has raised their voice. There is no hint of impending violence. A shout rings out from beyond the yard. A campus police officer for the University of Arizona is standing on the other side of a chain-link fence, yelling at Amy. Then he has a gun. Then he is shooting. Four shots, all hit her. The officer, Andrew Kisela, later states that he believed Hughes had raised her knife. His two colleagues cannot recall her doing so. They had come to the scene because they had been listening to Tucson Police Department radio and had heard a "check welfare" call for a woman with a knife at Amy's address. Looking for action, they had lighted out into the night.

Like Lula Brawner, Amy Hughes files suit under Section 1983, since Kisela is a state employee who counts as an official actor under that provision. The federal district court rules that Hughes's case cannot proceed because of a doctrine called "qualified immunity." It dismisses her case before any proceedings occur to gather evidence or hear and adjudicate the legal merits of her case. The Court of Appeals, however, in an unsigned judgment, reverses on the ground that there are issues of fact in dispute related to Kisela's defense. The officer appeals, now to the US Supreme Court. Without a hearing, without even allowing Amy Hughes to provide briefs on the case, the Supreme Court reverses and directs a result in favor of Kisela. The gist of its ruling is that it would not have been obvious to Kisela, given the facts just described, that his use of a firearm was unconstitutional. Lula Brawner at least got a day in court and some consideration of the merits of her case. Amy Hughes doesn't even get that.[2]

Amy Hughes's case was resolved two years before the parents of Sergio Adrián Hernández Güereca made their failed plea for restitution in the high court. To be sure, the Hernández family was unlike Hughes in that they were turned away not because of qualified immunity, but on the distinct legal ground that they had no right to sue a federal agent for the violence that needlessly ended their son's life.[3] In both instances, though, the plaintiffs did not just lose on the merits. They lost because the Court held that they simply had no right to present their case in court. There was no room in the courthouse for them. Having lost, they were left with nothing. In Webster Bivens's case, Justice John Marshall Harlan had recognized that "for people in Bivens' shoes, it is damages or nothing." So he had voted to allow Bivens's case to proceed. Not so now. Turning Hughes and the Hernández family away, the Court implicitly informed them that their security, their family, and their lives merited "nothing" by way of judicial response, and nothing by way of compensation or recognition.

Both cases reflect a larger move away from the robust judicial commitment to individual remedies that manifested in the 1950s onwards. Indeed, across all four lines of cases described in Chapter 3, the Supreme Court has curbed individual remedies. It has done so, moreover, in a rough lockstep fashion by imposing the same formal constraint on the availability of a remedy across otherwise quite disparate legal and practical contexts.

Beyond its outcome, the extraordinary manner in which Amy Hughes's case was resolved deserves some close scrutiny. The Supreme Court is a body with limited time and attention. In the Court's annual term ending in July 2020, for example, it issued only sixty-one opinions on the merits of legal questions that had been argued before the Justices, as well as six "summary reversals" akin to its treatment of Hughes's case. Under the Justices' own rules, petitions for review are not supposed to be granted unless they concern issues of national import or provide an opportunity to clarify a point of law on which the various lower courts have divided.[4] Mere error does not suffice to justify Supreme Court intervention, or at least it's not supposed to. In Hughes's case, however, the Supreme Court's unsigned opinion focused on whether the court of appeals applied the law correctly. It made no attempt to demonstrate that there was a question of general importance or a matter of national public policy salience. That is, it made no attempt to follow its own rules. Instead, the Court expended its putatively scarce, valuable time and work solely to shield a state officer who had used what was almost certainly unconstitutional

THE COLLAPSE OF CONSTITUTIONAL REMEDIES

violence against someone who had never been flagged as a threat. The Court did so, apparently, to instruct lower courts in no uncertain terms that they should do the same.

Amy Hughes's case, moreover, is not alone. Several other decisions with the same basic posture have come from the Roberts Court: A lower court allows a suit for constitutional remedies to proceed against a state official. The Court blocks it via a summary reversal in an unsigned opinion without giving victims of state violence a chance to brief or argue the matter.[5] This practice readily manifests the Court's seeming belief that victims of potentially unconstitutional state coercion have entitlement neither to a remedy nor a day in court. They are mere chaff, snarling the smooth operation of state coercion. More subtly, these cases articulate a new self-conception of the federal courts as shields for certain vectors of coercive state power. The federal judiciary, in other words, is an adjunct and aide to the despotic state—whatever the collateral damage.

The ensuing remedial equilibrium for victims of state violence cannot be understood, once more, without reference to the Article III blueprint and historical construction of the federal courts. As a historical, evolutionary matter, the remedial status quo is a result of the openness of the judiciary to shifting partisan forms of state-building supported by transient political coalitions. The institutional interests of the judiciary, meanwhile, have hardly provided sustenance for the continued vindication of individual rights since the 1970s. Rather, these institutional interests have tilted away from the project of remediation. The belief that our specific institutionalization of judicial independence—circa 1787 on the periphery of great empires and in the absence of any rooted central state—necessarily would lead to pressure toward conformity with law is a serious mistake. Its offspring lie elsewhere.

QUALIFIED IMMUNITY AS REMEDIAL COLLAPSE

Each of the four avenues for individual remediation fashioned from the 1950s onward has been narrowed of late. For each pathway, the Supreme Court has cabined the circumstances in which an official can be subject, directly or indirectly, to a penalty for unconstitutional conduct. Precise dynamics vary between the four paths, but a single general theme binds together these remedial constraints: A penalty—whether in the form of a damages award, an instruction to discard evidence, or an order to release a convicted defendant—can be issued for a constitutional violation only if a rights holder has demonstrated something extraordinary and beyond the pale. Only where it is crystal clear that the official did not just violate a constitutional rule, but acted in a blatantly and manifestly unconstitutional way, will a remedy be allowed. For simplicity's sake, this can be called a "fault" rule because it compels a result for the government unless the officer is shown to have acted with a flagrant and egregious disregard for constitutional law.

This idea of fault has snaked from one area of law to another. The central actor in its propagation has been the Supreme Court, not Congress. With one exception, the fault-based derogation of individual remedies has been accomplished via judicial decisions, not statutory text. But in the course of its trajectory, this new limit to remedies has attracted the support of Justices and judges from all parts of the political spectrum—suggesting that explanations turning on partisan projects for the judiciary cannot be the whole story.

Sometimes the Court has gone a step further. It has extinguished remedies entirely or changed the underlying substantive law to vitiate any possibility of recovery. In these moments, the aim of enabling state coercion free of judicial oversight overflows the realm of remedies to taint the substance of constitutional law itself. The result of all this is that the stories of Alexander Baxter, Amy Hughes, and the Hernández family are typical, not extraordinary. They embody the manner in which federal courts today view unconstitutional state violence at the end of the despotic state's long twentieth-century engorgement—an acceptable price of doing business.

The first remedial armature to emerge in the mid-twentieth century was the revival of Section 1983 as a font of damages for constitutional wrongs. But its importance on the ground was soon blunted by the development of a doctrine called qualified immunity. In practical effect, this latter doctrine bars plaintiffs from the courthouse unless they can demonstrate that their allegations meet a threshold of seriousness. Note, though, that qualified immunity is one among many barriers to relief. Its effect is echoed, for example, by parallel shifts in the substantive law of various individual constitutional rights. Getting rid of qualified immunity would address one bar to relief, but it would not necessarily change the actual outcomes of all cases in which it is presently applied.

How, though, did it come into being in the first place? Nine years after James Monroe's landmark suit, the Supreme Court first endorsed the idea that officials might be able to seek dismissal of a Section 1983 case because they had a "qualified" immunity, not just from final judgments but also from the very fact of being sued and having to defend themselves in court. The case, *Pierson v. Ray*, arose from the arrest of a group of interracial clergymen who had attempted to use a segregated Continental Bus terminal in Jackson, Mississippi. The ministers were arrested and quickly convicted for breach of the peace. Barely four months earlier, a group of Freedom Riders had been arrested under similar circumstances in Jackson and shipped off to the infamous Parchman prison. The clergymen, spared this gruesome carceral fate, sued separately the arresting officers and the sentencing judge. The Supreme Court, by an 8–1 decision, held that neither suit could proceed. Even though

Section 1983's text says nothing about any "immunities," Chief Justice Earl Warren—a former California governor and prosecutor before he became a generally liberal federal judge—held that the sentencing judge was absolutely immune from suit. Warren cited the rules for ordinary tort actions prevailing circa 1871, under which judges could not be sued. Then, more crucially, he turned to the suit against the police officers. Here, Warren's ruling was more narrowly calipered: The plaintiffs, Warren reasoned, were in effect tracing out the elements of an older common-law tort action of false imprisonment, which was usually lodged against private individuals. A defense to that old, nonconstitutional tort was that an arrest had been made in "good faith and probable cause." As in the common law, reasoned Warren, so too in an action alleging a constitutional wrong. Because the arrests had been made with probable cause, the plaintiffs had to lose.[6]

Pierson suggested that a defense of "good faith and probable cause" would avail only in actions of false imprisonment. Yet in a case decided in 1975, the Court—with the assent of all the liberal Justices—generalized *Pierson* beyond its immediate false-imprisonment context. If *Pierson* signaled the moral seriousness and high drama of the 1960s, the next case of *Wood v. Strickland* mainlined the most bathetic parts of the 1970s. A bunch of tenth-grade girls in Mena, Arkansas, spiked the punch served at an afterschool event with Right Time liquor. While the prank had no ill effects, the girls were still expelled for the semester. As Alexis de Tocqueville might well have predicted, they responded with a lawsuit. The Court ultimately dismissed their claim on qualified immunity grounds, finding that the school officials had acted in "good faith."

Litigation by disgruntled high-school pranksters, of course, was not then and is not now the mine-run of Section 1983 cases. So why did the Justices take up this unusual and relatively minor case? Recall that the Court has had discretionary control over the cases it selects since the 1925 Judges' Act. When Justices want to nudge the law in a particular way, they do so by picking a factually atypical case that makes their intended nudging harder to notice and easier to swallow. If you want to narrow a remedy that usually serves a good end, that is, do so in a case where the plaintiffs' concerns are ephemeral or frivolous. So it was that *Strickland*, a case about a jape rather than a body-blow, altered the nature of qualified immunity, pushing it from a rule tailored to a specific kind of claim (false arrest allegations) into a larger, general-purpose shield against suit or liability.[7]

Up to the *Wood v. Strickland* decision, qualified immunity had been a matter of good faith. The next important case abandoned this position in favor of one that looked at the seriousness of the constitutional wrong—a critical change for a subtle, lawyerly reason. It moved attention away from the particulars of the actual interaction and the actions of a specific defendant. Instead, it directed judges' and litigants' attention toward the arid and scholastic question of what the precedent held and how it related to the facts in the pleadings. This shift in the law thus spared the trial court judge charged with resolving the litigation in the first place from any need to consider the actions of the actual defendant. Turning qualified immunity from an inquiry into a case's facts into an abstract one about the law made it cognitively easier for judges to turn away plainly blameless victims of state violence without undermining their own self-conception as just and decent people.

The key case arose from federal, not state, malfeasance. In November 1968, Air Force management analyst A. Ernest Fitzgerald testified to Congress about cost overruns and technical difficulties in the development of the C5-A transport plane. In January 1970, he was fired. Believing himself the victim of politically motivated retaliation, Fitzgerald sued President Nixon and his aides for retaliation in violation of the First Amendment using a *Bivens* action. The Supreme Court bifurcated the case. It awarded the president an absolute immunity from civil suit while dismissing the suit against the presidential aides on qualified immunity grounds. The resulting 1982 judgment in *Harlow v. Fitzgerald*—joined by a bipartisan coalition of Justices—changed the doctrine profoundly. It shucked off any pretense of reading qualified immunity out of nineteenth-century tort law as *Pierson* had. Instead, it replanted that doctrine in nakedly pragmatic soil as a way of achieving certain policy outcomes. Henceforth, immunity from suit would attach unless a defendant had violated the "clearly established statutory or constitutional rights of which a reasonable person would have known."[8] Over time, this formulation would calcify. Later decisions interpreted the *Harlow* standard to mean that "all but the plainly incompetent or those who knowingly violate the law" would benefit from qualified immunity's shield.[9] In effect, the "good faith" exception for liability had been transformed into a dispensation in which only actual proof of "bad faith" merited a trial or damages for a constitutional wrong.

The Court subsequently made it even harder for plaintiffs like Amy Hughes to secure relief. It has insisted that, for the purpose of qualified immunity, "the law" be defined not in terms of a general principle but by reference to past court decisions applying a specific legal rule to either identical or very similar facts to the case at bar.[10] A plaintiff thus has to flag an earlier decision with legal and factual details paralleling hers to get a hearing. So when the Court defines a constitutional right as a general prohibition not a specific rule, the plaintiff is likely to founder. Even if that general norm's application to her case may be clear in the abstract, there is no earlier decision with identical facts.

This leads to bizarre litigation twists. In an illustrative 2002 case, an Alabama prisoner was handcuffed to an outdoor "hitching post" for two- and then seven-hour stretches, without bathroom breaks, while guards taunted him. The Supreme Court divided on whether qualified immunity applied, with a key point of division being the absence of precedent specifically concerning hitching posts.[11] It seems absurd to say that a gross and obvious kind of violence won't trigger liability simply because no one has tried it before—and yet that is what the doctrine suggests.

Perhaps the most important domain in which the Court has used vague standards rather than specific rules is the Fourth Amendment regime governing police violence. The key decision here came in 1989, when the Court took up the Section 1983 suit brought of Dethorne Graham. A diabetic man who suffered from an insulin reaction in a convenience store, Graham was stopped on leaving that store and beaten by police because he was thought (wrongly) to have been shoplifting. The Court defined the constitutional issue in terms of the Fourth Amendment, and then set forth an open-ended, multifactor standard. Consider all the facts, instructed the Court in a part of the opinion that (again) attracted no dissent, except one: Do not consider evidence of the officer's own subjective intent.[12] Of course, Graham lost under this legal rule: It was gerrymandered to exclude the evidence most likely to help the plaintiff, such as the officer's mistaken beliefs, biases, or outright animus.

In later cases, the amorphousness of the *Graham* standard has interacted with qualified immunity's demand for specificity to make it very hard for a plaintiff to identify a specific "clearly established" rule that has been violated. This demand for specificity, as much as the doctrine of qualified immunity writ large, has short-circuited Section 1983 as a constraint on police violence. This kind of subtle effect can stifle constitutional remediation very effectively without requiring that the Court explain or justify quite what it's doing—and without the public precisely understanding what has happened.

The absence of later precedent giving substance to the vague standards imposed in cases such as *Graham* will not necessarily improve with time. Rather, the absence of guiding precedent becomes self-replicating. No plaintiff can prevail without identifying an earlier case that is on point. As a result, courts can dismiss challenges to a particular constitutional violation on qualified immunity grounds repeatedly without ever getting to the constitutional merits or handing down a clear rule of law. This looping dynamic works in tandem with the economics of litigation and settlement in tort cases more generally. When the result of a tort case is reasonably foreseeable, parties have a strong incentive to avoid the costs of litigation and instead enter a settlement before filing suit. Trial happens only when plaintiff and defendant both think they will win—that is, in close cases. As a result, courts are rarely confronted with cases of clear unconstitutionality—so there will be few "clearly established" judicial answers even as to easy questions of law.

The fault-based logic of qualified immunity has further leaked into the substantive definition of some constitutional rights. Outside the policing context, the Fourth Amendment does not apply. Nevertheless, state officials often interact with people in ways that can imperil liberty or property. Prisons and jails are increasingly important contexts in which this happens. Public housing, benefits programs, and other elements of the social state can also be constructed around state surveillance and control. In all these contexts, officials are covered by the Constitution's Due Process Clause. The Court, however, has limited the contexts where the Due Process Clause offers meaningful protection in ways that echo the fault principle. In a pair of cases involving prisoners protesting first the loss of a model airplane kit and then a slip-and-fall—relatively trivial indignities of prison life—the Justices have required that a plaintiff show that the relevant defendant acted with a malign intent.[13] As a result of these decisions, when an official carelessly or recklessly deprives someone of liberty or property, there is no constitutional violation. And when a plaintiff cannot point to evidence of bad intent, an officer-defendant can easily escape suit by claiming to have acted with mere carelessness. The substantive constitutional law, in effect, echoes the evidentiary demand first crafted in qualified immunity law that officials act culpably before a constitutional remedy is allowed.

Two of the other four pillars supporting the individual remedies revolution—habeas and the exclusionary rule—have also been undermined by extensions of the same fault rule. This diffusion of doctrinal ideas from damages to these other, distinct contexts, moreover, resulted from a conscious transplantation of the basic fault model that underpins qualified immunity to new domains of law.

Recall that a second armature of individual remedies for constitutional rights is the 1867 habeas statute as glossed in *Brown v. Allen*—and now usually invoked by state prisoners asserting a constitutional flaw in their trial. Yet thanks to a combination of legislative changes and judicial glosses on the habeas statute, a prisoner challenging an unconstitutional trial must now make an almost impossible showing of fault to even get a hearing. The law here has a baroque complexity. Most prisoner-litigants are uncounseled and ill-resourced. They are easily tripped up by legal technicalities as to whether their claims have been properly presented and framed, or not. Even the Justices themselves often grant a hearing in a case, only to dismiss it as improvidently granted when they identify a previously hidden problem. By turning habeas law into a mare's nest of needlessly intricate tripwires and trapdoors, the Court and Congress have slanted the playing field against frivolous and merit-worthy claims alike.

The centerpiece of the doctrine, though, tracks qualified immunity's fault rule. A 1996 provision, enacted as part of the Anti-Terrorism and Effective Death Penalty Act, or AEDPA, imposes a threshold showing on habeas plaintiffs. To get a hearing on the merits of their constitutional claims, it says, petitioners must point to a ruling from a state criminal court in their case that is "contrary to, or involved an unreasonable application of, clearly established Federal law, as determined by the Supreme Court of the United States."[14] This 1996 measure has been crucial to the narrowing of habeas relief. It is both a product of, and also a platform for, judicial policy-making. Congress cribbed this 1996 standard from an early suggestion offered by Justice Clarence Thomas for limiting habeas relief.[15]

After the 1996 measure was enacted, moreover, the Supreme Court gradually ratcheted up its severity. While some of the ensuing decisions attracted dissents by liberal judges, many have been unanimous.[16] The Court's disdain for prisoner-litigants reached its peak in a decision holding that where a state court had not issued any ruling but simply dismissed a claim without explanation, the habeas applicant still had to imagine and rebut *all possible grounds* on which the state tribunal's rejection of a constitutional claim *might* have been made. There was no hiding the ball here. Instead, the Court was abundantly clear that only "extreme malfunctions in the state criminal justice system" justified relief.[17] Merely "ordinary" violations of the Constitution—notionally our fundamental law—do not count.

So too it goes with the exclusionary rule. In 1984, the Supreme Court conjured up a worry about the risk of chilling "objectively reasonable law enforcement activity" as a reason to carve out an exemption to the *Mapp* rule. The 1984 case, called *United States v. Leon*, focused on the problem of flawed warrants. Except in very rare cases, *Leon* said, evidence procured by an unconstitutionally defective warrant can still be used in court. (Unlike key decisions in the habeas and qualified immunity contexts, *Leon* provoked a fierce dissent by Justice Brennan.) Over time, however, the Court extended *Leon* to cover mistakes made not just by magistrates but also by police conducting searches without warrants.[18] Doing so, the

Justices expressly invoked the fault rule of qualified immunity as a template for their action.[19] The details of these ensuing cases are complex, but their effect is simple. It mirrors developments in the Section 1983 and the habeas domains. Absent a showing of bad faith or egregious error by the police, any evidence acquired through an unconstitutional search will be aired in a criminal trial.[20]

At the same time, the Court has made it easier for police to bypass the famous *Miranda* warnings by staging serial interrogations first without and then with warnings. At least where a defendant cannot show that the officer acted intentionally in circumventing the Constitution, police can use the second interview as a vehicle to recapitulate the information that had been gained in the first, putatively illegal interview.[21] The result of these accumulating changes to the law is striking: While formally an occasion for affirming the centrality of law to communal life, the criminal trial itself becomes an opportunity for the state to take away life or liberty using its own unlawful conduct.

What, finally, of *Bivens* actions against federal officials? As the *Fitzgerald* case indicated, qualified immunity applies in *Bivens* actions as much as in suits against state officials. Adding to the screening supplied by qualified immunity, the Supreme Court has trimmed the availability of litigants to bring a *Bivens* action in the first place. The case of Sergio Adrián Hernández Güereca is exemplary. Hernández's family, explained the Court, could not sue because the border was a "new" and "different" context from earlier *Bivens* decisions. And in any case, the Court sternly lectured the family, if there was to be a damages award against a federal official, that was for Congress to decide.[22] Likewise, the Court has also rejected constitutional claims brought by Muslim noncitizens detained allegedly because of their religion and national origin after the September 11, 2001, attacks.[23] The emotional tincture of these cases makes it easier for the Justices to issue rulings that have had the effect of casting wider doubt on *Bivens* across the board. Indeed, it has used another post-9/11 case as an opportunity to make much civil litigation more difficult to bring across the board.[24] These effects are well understood as the fruit, once again, of the 1925 Judiciary Act's grant of power to the Justices to select their own cases—here, to pick those fact patterns that facilitate, loudly or on the quiet, their general hostility to constitutional remedies for individuals subject to immediate state violence.

DEFERENCE AS THE ABSENCE OF REMEDIES

An additional barrier that hinders constitutional challenges to federal actions, whether through a *Bivens* action or any other device, is the judiciary's tendency first to defer to state officials' reasons whenever they proffer a minimally plausible justification sounding in public security or foreign affairs, and then to disallow discovery (e.g., depositions or requests for documents from the government) into the veracity of those justifications. Deference is an especially powerful force in the immigration context. It led the Court in 2018 to ignore, for example, President Trump's repeated and emphatic displays of animus against Muslims when evaluating his 2017 travel ban.[25] A year before that, it had also supported the dismissal of *Bivens* claims by immigrants detained on the basis of their religion—again without allowing the plaintiffs any discovery.[26] And in the *Hernández* case, the Court invoked the judiciary's relative disadvantage in evaluating the suit's "potential effect on foreign relations" as a reason to not allow the family to even litigate the case.[27] That there was scant evidence of any "effect of foreign relations" on the actual facts of the case hardly mattered.

Under these deference doctrines, the bench declines to credit the rights holder's evidence because the judge leans heavily on the government's version of events, and then disallows efforts to secure better evidence through the process of discovery. Barriers to the process of obtaining better evidence are sharpest in the national security context, where they have hindered most suits against even blatantly unconstitutional actions in the war against terror.

Bitter ironies arise from this doctrinal barricade against *Bivens* actions. Congress had, in fact, previously modified the statute that sets out when the federal government is liable for wrongs—say for the negligent driving of a federal employee—to clarify that it intended to preserve *Bivens* and even allow courts to extend its coverage of constitutional wrongs.[28] Solicitude for the legislative branch—never the Court's strong suit when the Justices disagree with Congress—is thus an improbable, almost perverse, basis for decisions taken on quite different grounds.

Further, the Court continues to present itself as a defender of individual rights even as it unravels effective rights enforcement regimes. For example, in the same decision in which they upheld President Trump's travel ban, the Justices made a great show of repudiating a decades-old precedent embracing President Roosevelt's 1942 internment of Japanese Americans. Even setting aside the manner in which the travel ban was grounded in much of the same xenophobic impulses as the internment, the Court (as I noted earlier) had just the year before eliminated *Bivens* remedies for federal detainees—in effect eliminating a critical constraint on lawless federal detentions akin to the internment of the 1940s. Even if a repeat of the Japanese American internment is now unlawful, the Court's jurisprudence of remedies has made such a measure extremely hard to challenge.

OTHER REMEDIAL RECESSIONS

Two other trends are worth picking out. First, all of the remedies discussed so far concern what happens after the Constitution has been violated. But what if you can anticipate unconstitutional violence? What if you could get to court before it happens and ask the court to shield you? The idea is not as outlandish as it sounds: Recall that in the late 1800s, the Republican-empowered federal courts developed the injunction as an instrument for national railroads to block unfriendly state rate regulation.[29] Could individual rights holders invoke that precedent and, like the advocates of school desegregation in the 1950s and 1960s, wield it as a shield?

In 1983, the Court made it clear that the answer was generally no where negative rights against coercion are at issue. Adolph Lyons was a twenty-four-year-old Black male living in Los Angeles who experienced an unprovoked police chokehold during a traffic stop. In his ensuing request for an injunction against all police chokeholds, Lyons alleged that the police in Los Angeles "regularly and routinely" used unjustified chokeholds. He explained that he feared that any future contact with the Los Angeles police would likely "result in his being choked and strangled to death without provocation, justification or other legal excuse." The Court rebuffed Lyons's claims on the grounds that he lacked "standing." A technical doctrine that regulates access to federal court, standing is a demand that a plaintiff in effect have some skin in the game. To establish standing, the Court explained, Lyons would have to show that a police officers in Los Angeles would *in fact* choke him during the next traffic stop.[30] Clearly, Lyons could not make such a showing of certain harm. (Consider in contrast Seila Law's ability to make a parallel showing that it was likely to be treated differently because of the way that an agency head could be removed—a question to which we return.). In individual rights cases at least, forward-looking injunctive relief is rarely available unless there is some certainty that a plaintiff will be subject to a repeat performance.

Another trend concerns the treatment of racial minorities. As the Court has disassembled the procedural vehicles by which minorities might challenge coercive state overreach, it has also made it well-nigh impossible to directly challenge the discriminatory deployment of official force.

A pair of cases decided in the late 1990s involving alleged discrimination by federal prosecutors and immigration officials illustrate the nearly insurmountable difficulty that racial minorities face when making discrimination claims. Under these decisions, minority litigants do not get discovery until they have identified a person of a different race similarly situated to them who was not targeted by the government. But to make this showing of a "similarly situated" person, it is often necessary to have access to the government's own enforcement files. These show who was targeted and who was not. Without them, a defendant often cannot point to a similarly situated person who authorities could have, but did not, arrest and charge. The result is a Catch-22 in which the threshold demand for a "similarly situated" showing cuts short most discrimination challenges to official action at the courthouse door.[31] For these victims of racial and ethnic discrimination, as Justice Harlan said, the remedy is once again "nothing."[32]

This barrier to equality-based challenges to policing, prosecutorial, and immigration practices, coupled with the fault rule that dominates individual remedies, means that victims of state violence have no effectual pathway for airing and challenging racist practices or policies that impose disproportionate costs on minorities. Challenges to discriminatory uses of state violence, whether by state or federal officials, have thus become very rare.

All this has not been the work of Congress. It is rather a result of decisions by the Court. Even where Congress has intervened, as in the habeas context, it largely followed cues offered by the Justices. At the same time, judicial action is guided not by settled law but questions of policy. When the Court constrains constitutional remedies nowadays, it thus appeals in the main not to some settled element of nineteenth-century common law, but to "considerations of public policy."[33] In other domains, the Justices say that these considerations are the exclusive province of the elected branches. When it comes to constitutional remedies, however, the Court has not hesitated to make its own normative judgments about when remedies are—or, more importantly, are not—available. It has seized the chance to exercise mastery over its own domain.

WAS THE COURT RIGHT TO CONSTRICT INDIVIDUAL REMEDIES?

But maybe these contractions are unproblematic. If remedies for individual constitutional harms are unnecessary, if they impose greater costs than benefits, or if they create new kinds of unfairness, then the remedial recession may well be justified. Are any of these justifications available?

To begin with, there's no reason to think that the need for constitutional remedies has diminished. The period from the 1970s onward has seen no secular decline in the size of the despotic state at either the state or federal level. If anything, state coercion has expanded with new and ferocious velocity. From the 1960s forward, the United States experienced an unprecedented rise in criminal violence as the postwar boom in young men collided with a world of shrinking labor-market opportunities, deteriorating central cities, and concentrated poverty.[34]

The national and state governments could have responded to this challenge in different ways. They chose coercion. In the policing domain, for example, the Crime Control Act of 1990 assigned $900 million to state-level drug enforcement. Then the 1994 Violent Crime Control and Law Enforcement Act authorized some $30 billion for state and local police over six years.[35] The more cops there are, of course, the greater the risk of unconstitutional violence. The same trends can be discerned in the development of federal coercive agencies. By the 1980s, the immigration agencies that brought Sergio Hernández to grief had established themselves as durable bureaucracies, capable of consistent and high levels of coercion.[36]

The Court has gestured at the "increasing professionalism of police forces" as a justification for remedial forbearance. Tellingly, the Justices have not said what exactly this means in practice (to say nothing of substantiating the assertion with anything as mundane as evidence). Professionalism might simply involve tighter command-and-control structures, with leaders who still tolerate a high level of violence. Or it might mean that officers develop more crime-solving expertise and hence need force less.[37] There is no necessary connection between professionalism and the reduction of coercion. Whatever its implicit definition, the Court has offered no evidence that unconstitutional violence is less a problem today than in the 1960s. The steady stream of high-profile deaths at police hands, from Michael Brown to George Floyd, is hard to square with the Court's blasé optimism about the soothing effects of police professionalism.

A potentially more substantial reason for scaling back remedies would look to what is best for society as a whole, rather than just looking only at the victim and the perpetrator. It would home in upon the post-1960 rise in criminal violence and the related possibility that a desirable level of socially beneficial state violence will be thwarted if officers are chilled by the prospect of constitutional remedies. Since *Harlow v. Fitzgerald*, the Court has wrung variations on this theme of chilling effects across the case law. At the same time, the Court has never cited any empirical evidence that police officers, who make up a large share of Section 1983 defendants, will in fact be overdeterred in the absence of the fault rule.

The Court's "chilling effect" theory would suggest that police are engaged now in socially optimal levels of violent coercion. This seems improbable, to say the least. Police forces are not typically subject to strict oversight. Unlike other agencies, they do not need to show that their policies are cost-benefit justified. Indeed, we simply do not know whether many common policing tactics, including *Terry* stops, have a meaningful effect on crime rates. Determining how much unlawful behavior there is using existing police records would be very hard, especially since these records are partial in ways that make the police look good. This problem is especially acute when it comes to estimating the effect of racial biases.[38] At the same time, a wealth of anecdotal and empirical evidence of excess illegal police violence is available. There is also a growing body of evidence showing the pervasiveness of constitutional violations in state criminal justice adjudication.[39] For the Court to rely on a bare intuition about chilling effects, it has to ignore that large body of evidence all suggesting that present coercive state action is nowhere near a social optimum.

But perhaps the chilling-effects justification for the fault rule can be explained without leaning on empirical evidence about the aggregate level of unlawful state violence. One defense in that vein runs as follows: Damages, if not the operation of the exclusionary rule or the habeas remedy, work against the officer individually. They force him in particular to bear the downside risk, and hence the costs, of his action. But when an officer takes a legally risky action and the action bears fruit, it is very likely that much of the ensuing benefits flow not to the officer but to the public at large. For instance, the officer might choose to give chase on a busy highway. If he catches the fleeing suspect, he has created some public safety that benefits everyone. As long as officials are not able to enjoy all of this upside, asking them to bear the downsides of those risks is not sensible. The asymmetry they experience between personally felt costs and benefits would result in officers shying away from legally risky actions that, in the scheme of things, are in fact justified.[40] Such forgone interventions may be especially deplorable at a time of rising criminal violence.

The problem with this justification is that it is, again, at odds with the facts. In the domain of state and local policing, officers almost never pay judgments out of pocket, when such judgments are awarded at all. Between 2006 and 2011, a study of forty-four of the country's largest jurisdictions found that officers financially contributed to settlements and judgments in just 0.41 percent of the approximately 9,225 civil rights damages actions resolved in the plaintiffs' favor. Their contributions amounted to just 0.02 percent of the more than $730 million spent by cities, counties, and states on these cases.[41] These statistics, of course, reflect a litigation context in which qualified immunity is already screening out all but the most extreme cases. It suggests that even when an officer is alleged to be "plainly incompetent" or "knowingly" breaks the law, they are unlikely to face financial penalties.[42] Thus, there simply is an asymmetrical burden on officers from tort judgments.

Yet another reason for doubting the risk-internalization justification for fault limits on constitutional remedies is that at both the national and the state level, the risk of constitutional harm does not fall evenly across the population. Minority racial and ethnic groups experience a glut of such harms in comparison with majority groups.[43]

Where the costs and benefits of coercion are spread so unevenly, there is reason to think that officials will not strike the "right" or "socially optimal" level of coercive activity, especially when the harms of official coercion fall on people unlike them. Officers are, to the contrary, likely to underestimate the harm accruing to minority communities even in the absence of forthright bias. Even trained physicians, after all, tend to underestimate African Americans' pain in clinical encounters.[44] It is likely that officials who are not as well trained are likely to do the same or worse. Quite apart from perceptual distortions, officials may be less attentive to the costs of coercion because they correctly anticipate that marginalized minorities will not be able to protest excessive force through democratic processes. Standing at the political periphery, therefore, may make people additionally vulnerable to the state's lash and gun.

A further argument for constraining remedies sounds in fairness terms. To sanction an official doing a difficult and strenuous job, even when they concededly err, without a very powerful reason to do so seems on its face unfair. It fails to account for the practical difficulties of her situation, and denies her the appropriate breathing room. In the long term, perhaps it breeds alienation and demoralization among those working for the government. The argument from fairness works best for damages awards under Section 1983 and *Bivens*. Neither the exclusionary rule nor the grant of habeas corpus relief involves a specific official being singled out for a personal opprobrium or setback. It is thus hard to see why they would implicate fairness to the officer. But even in the damages context, fairness worries are difficult to credit. In respect to policing, where the largest damages awards are likely to arise, insurance coverage for damages awards is known to be pervasive. An official can bargain for insurance to cover her expected costs. A state employer offering a position without insurance should expect applicants for jobs to search for alternative positions or demand an implicit wage discount.

Liability might alter the terms of those contracts. But this does not render them unjust.

Officials' shield against liability is often airtight in another way. A 2016 study of sixty-two large law enforcement agencies found that twenty-six never paid damages awards. Rather, those funds were drawn from a central fund common to the city or county as a whole.[45] Under this arrangement, a police department that routinely incurs large money judgments because of officer misconduct has no financial reason to change its ways. Taxpayers are footing the bill for their mistakes. Perhaps a mayor or county commission could pressure the police to alter their practices, but their power to do so is often uncertain. A police union may be too powerful, or a mayor too vulnerable to public criticism, for this to work. Mayors often depend on police to achieve policy successes that a sclerotic civilian bureaucracy cannot deliver. Under these circumstances, no fairness concern arises— because liability will never hit home.

Perhaps the fault-based regime aims to promote fairness in a different way. Perhaps it aims to ensure that officers have actual notice of what rules they cannot violate. If so, it is ill-suited to that end. In *Kisela v. Hughes*, for example, the Court framed the qualified immunity inquiry in terms of the intricacies of earlier cases. But street-level bureaucrats such as police are unlikely to know these details. Training for police, for example, focuses on big-picture principles, not granular jurisprudential details.[46] If the Court's ambition is to ensure that officers have fair warning of liability risk, it is doing an exceedingly poor job.

Finally, an opponent of remedies might point to the risk of a political backlash that in the end will undermine remedies' availability. Perhaps the most cogent argument along these lines came from the brilliant scholar William Stuntz in a series of powerful articles and a posthumous book. Stuntz suggested that the midcentury explosion in individual rights triggered a backlash among state legislatures.

Restrained from changing criminal process, he suggested, legislators piled up new criminal penalties, making conviction easier and along the way filling more and more prisons.[47] But other scholars have pointed out that the changes to substantive criminal law that Stuntz underscored *preceded* new criminal process rights and remedies rather than following them.[48] More recent work has also uncovered larger political economy dynamics that explain overcriminalization without reference to Stuntz's backlash theory.[49] The risk of backlash, in other words, has not been proved. It is a speculative, not a plausible, basis for justifying the collapse of constitutional remedies.

COLLAPSE'S CAUSES

The causes of remedial collapse are rooted in the numerous vulnerabilities of the Article III blueprint and the historical construction of the judiciary. Collapse is first a direct result of the successful appointment of judges adverse to late-twentieth-century racial reconstruction. Whereas new judges through the 1950s and 1960s were in effect delegates of a Democratic Party faction, subsequent judicial nominees have been advanced by presidents because of very different policy commitments. The institutional interests of the judiciary, at the same time, have imposed no friction on this retreat, and may have even accelerated it. To blame the collapse of constitutional remedies merely on the pattern of judicial appointments—important as those were—is hence to miss the enabling and abetting effects of judicial independence.

In the late 1970s and 1980s, as the Warren Court gave way to the Burger and the Rehnquist Courts, an ideological sea change overturned the judiciary. In a stark pivot away from President Lyndon Johnson's Great Society, Republican presidential candidate Richard Nixon promised "law and order" through policing. A cascade of violent urban riots started in the Watts neighborhood of Los Angeles in August 1965. Nixon and his allies argued that civil rights liberalization was to blame for these riots and the sharp violent crime rises of the era. Their anodyne law-and-order slogan, racially neutral on its face, conjured up a racialized package of anxieties about civil disorder, mandatory busing, integrated schools, and uncontrolled crime. Rather than contesting these tropes, Democrats responded by desperately trying to mimic and even outbid Republicans. The Overton window moved. National media joined in, blaming the civil rights movement and African Americans more generally, for urban riots and lawbreaking.[50] By 1973, crime had crowded out civil rights in the national Democratic Party's agenda as well as the Republican one.[51]

At the same time, a subtle change in social mores was afoot. The historian Daniel Rodgers has suggested that a manifestly more diverse nation—where women, African Americans, and migrant groups were increasingly visible and vocal—prompted a public backlash. The shared ideal of a collective good gave way in the 1970s into "something smaller, more voluntaristic, fractured, easier to exit, and more guarded." Rodgers further argued that "conceptions of human nature . . . thick with context, social circumstances, institutions, and history gave way to conceptions of human nature that stressed choice, agency, performance, and desire."[52]

Although it is hard to draw any firm and clear causal connection from these larger trends and the specifics of law, the judiciary's retreat from individual remedies is certainly of a piece with the larger trend that Rodgers flagged. As with the fracturing of the social that he described, the march away from remedies reflects an increasing unwillingness to recognize the collective, solidaristic implications of governing. It is a denial that public safety and similar goods are produced in ways that benefit us all, but with costs that often fall in uneven, perhaps unjust ways. It is a rejection of the idea that we, as a society, are all in this together.

Additionally, the move away from individual remedies reflected the shifting racial politics in the 1970s. National and local armatures of the despotic state had both been associated with a candidly racist project of state-building. Slave patrols, the Fugitive Slave Acts, and the Chinese Exclusion Acts were its tools. The despotic apparatus of official power developed through the twentieth century at the state and federal level, and aimed in large part toward the preservation and extension of racially hierarchical accounts of the state. This state apparatus did so by containing African Americans in urban centers while keeping non-White and Hispanic populations on the outer rim of an international border. To be sure, the individual rights revolution of the 1950s and 1960s had been one element of a larger judicial campaign to unravel White supremacy. Its reversal in the 1970s allowed the reassertion of racial hierarchy working through various forms of the despotic state.[53] Nixon himself made this connection when he pungently described one of his own political commercials as "all about law and order and the damn Negro–Puerto Rican groups out there."[54]

Remedial recession both reflected and helped construct a new racial politics. It first tightly constrained one important avenue— lawsuits—through which racial injustice could be made salient to the public. Black victims of discrimination appeared with decreasing frequency in the law reports. In lieu of those victims, conservative Justices started to write opinions in the early 1970s in which the central victim of American racism was the White man disadvantaged by affirmative action in favor of either women or racial minorities. In so doing, they would plant intellectual seeds for a culture of White victimhood that would come to full and visceral flower more than forty-five years later.[55]

It was against this larger social context that Nixon made his four appointments to the Supreme Court and also replaced about half of the lower court bench. Nixon's appointees pushed for the constitutional deregulation of state and federal criminal justice agencies. They expressed open "hostility to fair process norms that impair the state's capacity to detect and punish the factually guilty."[56] The trend in appointments continued in subsequent Republican administrations. Presidential advisor and subsequent Chief Justice William Rehnquist encouraged President Reagan to appoint "strict constructionists" to the federal courts, who "will generally not be favorably inclined toward claims of either criminal defendants or civil rights plaintiffs."[57]

This strategy of pursuing a policy goal indirectly through the courts, of course, is nothing new. Just as the Republicans of the 1870s and the Democrats of the 1940s had relied on the federal courts to pursue policies that they could not attain directly through Congress, so the post-Nixon Republican coalition pursued its agenda of deregulating state coercion through the courts. The House of Representatives, indeed, remained in Democratic hands until the 1994 elections—making judicial appointments an especially alluring path for policy change on the Republican side. A law-and-order agenda that appealed to the Republican electorate was implemented through a neutral and legalistic channel in a way that appeased the party's base while allowing some deflection of criticism on racial or distributive grounds. The argot of "strict constructionism" tended by Nixon's judges mattered, in this context, not because it described any consistent interpretative strategy (it didn't, and doesn't now) but rather because it provided a way to wrap regressive steps away from the Second Reconstruction in neutral words and plausible deniability. Federal courts, in other words, are useful policy instruments because they permit politicians to send plural, perhaps conflicting, messages to different constituencies about their ambitions. In this way, the use of the federal judiciary as a policy instrument undermines clear lines of democratic accountability.

In the 1970s, therefore, the structure of judicial independence—and its reliance on after-the-fact protections—was an invitation to partisan instrumentalization. Unlike earlier periods, there was no need to tweak the jurisdiction of the courts to achieve this effect. It was not until 1996 that the Republican Congress passed, and President Clinton signed, laws that stripped or narrowed jurisdiction to hear prisoner cases, immigration, and postconviction challenges to state criminal sentences. As we have seen, even these measures tended to work with the grain of judicial preferences.

Yet at the same time, the wave of partisan appointments starting under the Nixon administration cannot be the whole story. Recall that *Pierson v. Ray* was an opinion by Chief Justice Earl Warren, from which only Justice Douglas dissented. Habeas's narrowing has had consistent bipartisan support. Voting in *Harlow v. Fitzgerald* and *United States v. Leon* similarly did not break along precise partisan lines. Rather, there is circumstantial evidence that Justices of varied political stripes have long viewed constitutional remediation as problematic because of concerns about the resulting caseload imposed on federal judges. The gatekeeping fault rule did not emerge solely at the behest of Justices appointed by presidents centrally concerned with crime control.

This bipartisanship is likely best explained by shared institutional loyalties within the judiciary. Worries about judges' caseload in particular have long loomed large in the judicial consciousness. In 1971, for example, Chief Justice Warren Burger created a Study Group on the Caseload of the Supreme Court to consider "backlogs in judicial business, inadequacies in judicial performance, and potential reforms in judicial organization or administration." This Study Group, and its successors, the Commission on Revision of the Appellate System and the Hruska Commission, could not get Congress to act. But they nonetheless embodied and reinforced judges' widely shared sense of a caseload crisis in the offing.[58] Reflecting on the courts' experience from the 1960s through the 1980s, Chief Justice Rehnquist later remarked on "the great increase of judicial business handled by the federal courts," and "the increasing complexity of the issues now handled by the federal courts."[59] To be sure, he did not pick out habeas cases or civil rights suits under Section 1983 explicitly. He did not need to. Both these kinds of cases had experienced explosive growth since the 1950s. They were plainly a large part of the perceived caseload problem.

Justices since the 1960s have repeatedly resisted constitutional remedies because of these worries. Importantly, liberal Justices have expressed the same caseload-related anxieties about constitutional remedies as their conservative colleagues. In the *Bivens* case itself, for example, Justice Hugo Black pressed a concern with "frivolous" suits in his dissent. Then in 1983, Justice Byron White argued for a fault-based limitation in suppression remedies on the ground that it would yield a "reduction in the number of cases which will require elongated consideration of the probable-cause question."[60] He then cited the qualified immunity standard as an instrument for managing the flow of Fourth Amendment cases to the federal courts. Both Justices Black and White, it should be noted, often voted as liberals while on the Court.

The pattern has continued during the Rehnquist and Roberts Courts. Discussing qualified immunity in 2004, liberal Justice Stephen Breyer complained that "courts' dockets are crowded" because of Section 1983 cases.[61] In *Harlow v. Fitzgerald*, the majority opinion written by conservative Justice Lewis Powell expressed concern about the volume of Section 1983 cases.[62] None of the liberals who joined his opinion raised any quibble on this point. Then, in 1989 Justice Anthony Kennedy expressed his concern about the "disproportionate amount of [judicial] time and energy" required for postconviction review.[63] In 2006, the whole Court had endorsed a concern about a "constant flood of alleged failures" to follow the

Fourth Amendment that would overwhelm the courts with exclu-sionary motions.[64] And in 2020, Justice Samuel Alito would complain at length in a dissent to a (fleeting) victory for a habeas prisoner about the "outsized place" of habeas cases on federal dockets.[65] His complaint was old, the vessel new.

Liberal or conservative, new or old, Justices are likely to take, or at least vocalize, an institutional perspectives on docket and caseload management without regard to ideological priors. The judiciary's influence, after all, depends on its ability to express its preferences though litigation—rather than being swamped by appeals from lower courts. In the 1920s, Chief Justice William Howard Taft had insisted on the Supreme Court's control of its own docket as a way of managing overload concerns. Similarly, the late-twentieth-century judiciary has responded to a perceived excess of cases by barring certain plaintiffs at the courthouse door.

The Court, in short, had both the means and the motive to trans-late its institutional autonomy into a fault-based regime of reme-dial limits. Historical and contemporaneous evidence suggests that judges define their interests in institutional terms, and that man-aging the federal courts' caseload is central to their own conception of this institutional interest. All this suggests that there is no *necessary* connection between judicial independence and the protection of in-dividual rights. The two can work together, or they can come apart. The late twentieth and early twenty-first centuries hence represent an era in which the realization of judicial independence may well have done more to harm than help the cause of individual rights.

CHAPTER 5

. . .

Remains

The past, the present and the future, are not discrete and cut off from one another. . . . We live the simultaneity of that entanglement.

Claudia Rankine[1]

CAROL ANNE BOND was thrilled when her best friend Myrlinda Haynes announced she was pregnant. The shine came off the news when Bond learned that it had been *her* husband, and not Haynes's, who had fathered the child. Bond was a microbiologist then working for the chemical manufacturer Rohm and Haas. She stole 10–chloro10H–phenoxarsine from her employer and ordered via Amazon some potassium dichromate. Combined, these chemicals can cause toxic harm with even small topical application. Over several months, Bond applied this chemical blend to Haynes's home doorknob, car door handles, and mailbox. But Haynes noticed. She avoided serious harm and persuaded postal inspectors to investigate. Bond was caught in the act and charged in federal court with mail theft and violations of the 1993 Chemical Weapons Convention.

In federal court, Bond challenged this last count because it violated a "principle of federalism." Her case traveled to the Supreme Court twice: First on whether she had the ability to press the states' interests in limited government power through her own criminal case, and second on whether the criminal elements of the Convention reached her conduct. Both times she won. She first gained the right to press a structural constitutional complaint in federal court. Then she got her sentence vacated. The Court, with no liberal dissents, ruled for Bond on the ground that the Convention had to be interpreted in light of federalism concerns that *might* be compromised if the Convention reached her case. It was not federalism, but its inky penumbra, that shielded Bond from federal prison.[2]

Bond's case is not unique. It shows how the federal courts continue to provide a shield against certain threats of state coercion, albeit under the rubric of vindicating the Constitution's structural principles. The most important of these unwritten norms are federalism and the separation of powers. The first concerns the relationship of the federal government to the several states. The second involves the relationships between the three branches. In federalism and separation-of-powers cases, a private litigant often asserts an interest in a structural principle of government, not an individual right, as a way to stave off a prospect of government coercion down the road. These cases rarely concern the immediate inflection of violence, like Alexander Baxter's, Sergio Hernández's, and Amy Hughes's suits. Rather, they are filed by litigants who want to avoid government regulation entirely, and not just the use of immediate state violence.

Bond, for example, asserted in effect a right to be free of regulation under the 1993 Chemical Weapons Convention. Her structural constitutional suit is typical in as much as she was not called upon to navigate the threshold screening rules that individual rights holders have to overcome. There was no threshold demand that she demonstrate that the constitutional error at issue was clearly established or otherwise obvious. Nor did she need to point to a right to action. Indeed, Bond was not asked to show that application of the 1993 Chemical Weapons Convention to her case in fact fell beyond the federal government's treaty-making powers. Rather, the Court's holding rested on a prophylactic logic. She prevailed despite not making a showing that Congress lacked power to criminalize her conduct because of the value of upholding structural principles beyond her case.

In one way, though, Carol Anne Bond's case was atypical. Most structural constitutional challenges are not filed by an individual trying to stave off arrest and incarceration like Carol Anne Bond. It is far more common for structural constitutional principles to be asserted, especially in the Supreme Court, by a regulated entity. This is often a corporation such as Seila Law; sometimes, it is a political subdivision such as a state. The reason is that most applications of federalism and the separation of powers restrict the scope or subject matter of government regulation. They tend to concern *what* the state can regulate, and not *how* it acts directly against individuals. Structural constitutionalism litigation is therefore most useful to entities wishing to shuck off a regulatory burden, not those seeking to challenge a discrete act of state violence. Federalism and separation of powers challenges are accordingly lodged mostly by entities with an interest in limiting regulatory power, and with the resources to pull off a sustained litigation campaign to this end. The Court's choice to facilitate the litigation of structural constitutional claims, even as it severely rations rights against immediate state coercion, has a predictable distributive tilt. It is a choice to favor one class of litigants over another.

The categories of structural constitutional principles on the one hand, and the negative rights that Baxter, Hernández, and Hughes wanted to vindicate on the other, do not cover the waterfront of constitutional challenges. These two boxes leave out a class of what might be called individual rights against regulation. Gun rights under the Second Amendment, free speech and religious liberty arguments under the First Amendment, constraints on government "takings" under the Fifth Amendment—all these tend to tend to work as shields against regulation, not protections against immediate acts of physical coercion.

Increasingly, such rights against regulation are used to carve out domains of private autonomy for property or piety. In 2019, for example, the Court removed a significant procedural barrier to land-owners who wished to challenge a taking of their real property in federal, rather than state, court. Two years later, it created a consti-tutional right for land owners to keep out unwelcome voices—such as union organizers on a factory floor—from their domain, in effect transforming an ancient common law of trespass into a constitutional mandate.[3] Property owners, indeed, almost always prevail in the Roberts Court. The latter has also buttressed the right of religious institutions to refuse to comply with regulatory mandates, such as contraception-related insurance rules and antidiscrimination man-dates.[4] Litigants invoking these rights are a mix of individuals and entities such as corporations. A drift away from individual and to-ward corporate litigants can be detected here too.[5] These individual rights cases, moreover, do little to protect the vulnerable from direct state coercion. To the contrary, the Roberts Court's decisions on the Fifth Amendment and religious liberty tend to increase the vulner-ability of the socially marginal to new forms of private violence and discrimination.

So we come full circle from the late nineteenth century: The allocation of attention under Article III is powerfully influenced by transient partisan agendas because of the failure of Hamilton's presuppositions. These partisan forces are sieved through appointments and (more infrequently) jurisdictional reforms. The mid-twentieth-century dispensation favoring racial—and hence socioeconomic—egalitarian values against Jim Crow and its variants has been in decline since the 1970s. Its successor, whether wrapped in the argot of "law and order" or "strict constructionism," has blessed the despotic state with a new lease on life. By contrasting its approach to the despotic state with its quite different attitude toward the regulatory and social state, the payoff from partisan investments in the judiciary snaps into stark perspective. The Court now has an impressive capacity to engage in redistribution between social classes in ways that are often invisible to the public. Its actions can nevertheless have enduring effects on the forms and nature of state power.

WHAT REMAINS IS STRUCTURE

Federalism concerns the powers of the states in relation to the federal government. Carol Anne Bond is not the only person to use it as a shield from the state's regulatory reach. On a morning in March 1992, Alfonso Lopez Jr., a twelfth-grader at Edison High School in San Antonio, Texas, arrived at school carrying a concealed .38-caliber handgun. He had been paid forty dollars to deliver the weapon for use in a "gang war." Like Bond, Alfonso was prosecuted in federal court, this time under the Gun Free School Zones Act. And like Bond, he was able to persuade a majority of Justices that this federal criminal law fell outside the national government's powers.[6]

Then, in fall 1995, a woman named Christy Brzonkala was raped by fellow students Antonio Morrison and James Crawford soon after enrolling in Virginia Polytechnic Institute. When the university failed to sanction either man—both were on its football team—Brzonkala sought damages in federal court under Title IX of the 1972 Education Amendments. At the Supreme Court, she was rebuffed. Echoing Lopez's case, the Court reasoned that the federal Congress had no business regulating gender-based violence because it fell within the exclusive "police powers" of the states.[7]

These individuals' structural challenges are exceptions rather than the rule. Federalism principles are more commonly invoked by collective entities such as states. Consider, for example, the repeated challenges targeting the Affordable Care Act in 2011, 2015, and 2021. The most important of these was decided in 2011. There, acting at the behest of both state litigants and private plaintiffs, the Court found that Congress lacked power to impose an insurance mandate except as a conditional tax, and struck down a major expansion of Medicaid as an exercise of improper coercion by the federal government.[8] This was not the first time that states had used federalism to challenge national regulation (although the Affordable Care Act case is the rare case in which states used litigation to fend off having to accept dollars from the federal government). Through the 1990s, federalism interests were often invoked to draw tight boundaries on the power of the federal government to enforce antidiscrimination mandates on the states via damages actions. These limits redounded to the detriment of older and disabled workers turfed out of state employment.[9] Subsequently, federalism has been invoked to a variety of deregulatory ends not just by states themselves but by private actors too. For instance, in one case, it was applied to bar one state's courts from adjudicating a class-action dispute against national companies engaged in dubious business across several states. This in effect derailed an effective aggregation of small claims, and undermined protections for consumers.[10]

An important continuity between these otherwise disparate federalism cases is the way in which they tend to limit the federal government's regulatory reach. Indeed, it is the prospect of such constraint that makes federalism alluring for litigants as varied as Alfonso Lopez, Antonio Morrison, and the state of Alabama. The

Court has posited that promotion of a structural principle in these cases promoted individual liberty from governmental coercion. This is doubtful. Defendants such as Alfonso Lopez and Carol Anne Bond obtained, to be sure, a temporary reprieve from criminal liability. But both remained vulnerable to state prosecution after the federal government's indictment had been dismissed. Moreover, it is relatively straightforward to write a new federal statute that covers their cases. Indeed, after the *Lopez* decision, Congress amended the statute at issue there to include the requirement that the firearm in question had traveled in interstate commerce. That new version easily passed constitutional muster, and remains on the books.[11] Given the ease of their circumvention, federalism decisions such as Lopez's are likely to have a main effect of increasing vulnerability to violence and discrimination at the hands of state officials and private actors. Plainly and painfully, Christy Brzonkala and others were left tragically exposed to sexual violence that state authorities have neither the will nor the wherewithal to address. Equally, as a result of the Court's 2012 decision on the Affordable Care Act, some fourteen states declined new Medicaid funds and left many of their lower-income citizens without meaningful access to insurance coverage. The net effect of such federalism decisions is the exposure of already vulnerable communities to new forms of vulnerability to state and private violence. Across these cases, federalism principles have done less to advance the interests of states as such, and more to redistribute entitlements between more or less favored constituencies.

Provision of individual remedies against state coercion has no kindred effect on marginalized groups. Making damages available for state violence, or allowing exclusion or habeas relief, may lead to officials forbearing from certain kinds of violence and on occasion specific defendants being released from custody—but even this is far from certain. At the edge, state coercion is a bit more costly. But this is highly unlikely to yield meaningful increases in criminal violence.

Rare indeed will be the case in which a defendant is freed due to a constitutional ruling and then goes on to commit another violent crime. Because of the sheer size and capacity of the despotic state, officials are almost never entirely disabled from effectual action by legal bars to specific forms of coercion.

Rather, a legal regime in which the state can reliably resort to unlawful violence without fear of a reprimand is going to be one in which trust in the state and willing obedience to the law are in deficit. As policing agencies come to rely on violence and unlawful tactics, they lose the trust of their communities. It is also plausible that the ready availability of illegal means of acquiring evidence, forcing confessions, and pressuring individuals into confessions will lead to higher rates of false positives in charging decisions. The investigative skills that would produce more accurate outcomes also may wither away in a process called deskilling. By making violence cheaper, eliciting community distrust and deadening the incentive to acquire investigative skills, the Court participates in a profoundly unhealthy and harmful policy dynamic.

Federalism received much attention during the time that William Rehnquist was Chief Justice, but has waned somewhat during John Roberts's tenure. As befits a lawyer who cut his teeth in the executive branch—and who has seven colleagues who similarly worked as young lawyers in Article II positions—Roberts has led a Court that has vigorously pursued its own account of separation-of-powers principles. A primary beneficiary of this trend has been private entities subject to regulation by the government—and not just Seila Law. In 2010, a Nevada accounting firm, Beckwirth & Watts LLP, prevailed in a constitutional challenge to an element of the Sarbanes-Oxley Act's schema for dealing with post-Enron accounting chicanery. The Public Company Accounting Oversight Board (PCAOB) had issued a report critical of the firm's accounting audit procedures. Before PCAOB could do anything more, Beckwirth & Watts sued to stop regulatory action on the ground that the president lacked complete power to remove the PCAOB's members.

The Constitution itself does not speak of a removal power, let alone exclusively vesting it in the president. But starting in the 1980s, conservative lawyers in and around the White House started to develop a theory of the "unitary executive." At its inception, this constitutional theory pivoted on the president's unstated, but putatively absolute, authority to remove any official within the executive. Over time, it came to assume other, more sinister colorations.[12] A 5–4 majority of the Court embraced this theory's removal-related element to the PCAOB. This had the effect of hindering, although not entirely derailing, efforts to regulate Beckwirth & Watts. The Court's ruling did not depend, however, on the specifics of that case, or the risk that the alleged constitutional flaw in the agency's organization chart had in fact influenced the way Beckwirth & Watts had been regulated. Rather, the majority opinion written by Chief Justice Roberts developed an elaborate, counterfactual account of the circumstances in which the president might wish to remove a PCAOB member but would be unable to do so because of the statutory limits on the removal power.[13] The mere possibility that a constitutional problem could have—hypothetically, at least in principle—influenced the firm's treatment was enough to open the courthouse door.

Similar to the removal-power litigation is the case filed by one Raymond Lucia. He was an investment advisor who marketed a retirement savings strategy called "Buckets of Money" with a slideshow that the Securities and Exchange Commission (SEC) considered less than candid. Lucia was charged under the federal Investment Advisers Act in a proceeding conducted by an administrative law judge. These are not Article III judges. They are instead selected by SEC staff and have a limited tenure. Lucia argued that the Constitution's rules for how officers of the United States can be appointed prohibited this arrangement. As in the cases involving the Consumer Finance Protection Bureau (CFPB) and the PCAOB, the Court once more sided with the regulated party. It held that the administrative judge who had heard Lucia's case had been improperly appointed. As in removal cases, its ruling did not depend on how Lucia himself had actually been treated, or whether a different adjudicator would have behaved differently. It rather turned on a hypothetical state of affairs in which the appointment mechanism might have influenced the outcome of a proceeding.[14] And once again, there was no call for Lucia to show that the constitutional error was an especially clear or egregious one.

All these challenges by regulatory entities are joined by commonalities that distinguish them from instances in which the federal courts are asked to remedy discrete instances of state violence. To begin with, regulatory challenges are not characterized by any threshold sorting of cases based on the quality or severity of constitutional violation. Nothing in these cases resembles the fault demand of qualified immunity, postconviction habeas review, and the exclusionary rule. None of the litigants in these structural constitutional challenges had to demonstrate that the constitutional problem presented by the challenged regulation was particularly egregious. To the contrary, these challenges proceed absent evidence that the constitutional violation caused them any harm. In the removal cases, the Court has hence granted relief by reasoning that the president's constitutional authority might be hindered in some hypothetical case not before the Court.

There is all the practical difference in the world between a regime in which a plaintiff has to show that a constitutional violation is clearly established and one in which a plaintiff is relieved from the burden of even pointing to a constitutional violation on the facts of her case. The first kind of plaintiffs will have a much harder time getting into federal court than the second. Choosing between these procedural regimes, therefore, is a way of allocating the valuable public good of constitutional adjudication between the two groups of plaintiffs.

To see this clearly, contrast the treatment of Adolph Lyons and Seila Law. Recall that Adolph Lyons was not entitled to an injunction—indeed, not entitled to get into court—unless he could show with certainty that the Los Angeles Police Department would place him in a chokehold once again. Even the grave likelihood of such terrible violence was simply not enough to make a "harm" that licensed litigation moving forward.[15] Not so in the structural constitutional context. Seila Law argued that the Constitution was violated by a provision that limited the president to firing the CFPB's chief. Under that provision, the president could remove that person only on a showing of "inefficiency, neglect of duty, or malfeasance in office." But there was no evidence that the president in the White House then wished to fire the current director for any reason at all. To the contrary, at the time of the litigation, the CFPB was run by a 2018 Trump appointee, Kathleen Kraninger. Even without the removal power, the White House also had at hand a wide array of instruments for influencing administrative agency action, including Kraninger's. So it is not even clear that the Court's expansion of its removal authority made any real difference.[16] Any harm from an alleged Article II violation in Seila Law's case, therefore, resided in a heaven of legal concepts distant from the actual facts of how Seila had been treated by the CFPB.

There is another way in which the Supreme Court modulates the intensity of threshold screening rules so as to disable individual rights bearers while empowering litigants with structural constitutional claims. In both kinds of litigation, rights holders can identify a general class of government conduct and seek a remedy that runs against a whole category of state action. A class-based challenge of government conduct raises an important procedural question: How frequently must a constitutional violation occur within a class before a court allows a class-wide remedy? Must a litigant point simply to one instance of unconstitutionality out of dozens or hundreds of cases, or must he demonstrate that such illegality is more pervasive? Must they show that the law is sometimes, or pervasively, unconstitutional?

The Court has given different answers to this question in individual rights and structural constitutionalism cases. Consider again the *Lyons* decision: The force of Adolph Lyons's argument was that African American men, as a class, were persistently subject to chokeholds by the LAPD, and that an injunction in his case would mitigate this harm to the entire class. The Court, though, refused to allow his case to move forward without evidence that *every* encounter between the police and someone like Lyon ended in a chokehold.

In contrast, the Court invalidates statutes on structural constitutional grounds even though a substantial fraction of the statute's applications are plainly constitutional. In the 2012 Affordable Care Act case, for instance, a majority of Justices found that Congress lacked power under the Commerce Clause of Article I to impose a health-insurance mandate on individuals because doing so involved the regulation of "inactivity." The Court breezed past evidence that a majority of those subject to the health-insurance mandate regularly used (and hence somehow financed) healthcare in every calendar year. It instead focused on the theoretical possibility of inaction by a minority of those covered by the healthcare law as a means to finding the whole law unconstitutional.

Across these cases, therefore, the Court subtly modulated the evidentiary burden on litigants: Lyons had to show that constitutional violations were frequent; the states and private parties challenging the Affordable Care Act prevailed even though the alleged constitutional overreach was plainly limited to a subset of the statute's applications.

A third way in which the rules for individual rights and structural constitutional principles diverge is in the scope of the remedy actually granted. Remedies for rights against the coercive state tend to be narrow and granular. Only the specific person asserting a right gets an award of money damages, the exclusion of evidence, or a conviction thrown out. In contrast, in the structural context, remedies are wholesale. For example, in ruling on the CFPB or the PCAOB's removal provision, the Court did not attempt to limit the remedy to the litigants at bar. Rather, it invalidated certain portions of the agencies' founding statutes. Similarly, the remedy in Raymond Lucia's case was not particular to him. His case instead had the effect of changing the way in which the SEC's administrative law judges were appointed more generally.

None of these differences between the political economy of rights and structural litigants are prominent on the surface of opinions. The Justices rarely allude to them explicitly. They likely escape the public's attention. Their very subtlety suggests how the Justices can silently place their thumb on the scales, quietly favoring some litigants over others. Constitutional litigation as a whole is, in short, redistribution in all but name.

WHY THE DIVERGING PATHS OF RIGHTS AND
STRUCTURE CASES MATTERS

The Constitution is a repository of our plural histories. Sedimented and subterranean, the normative and policy commitments of different historical moments are now and again scooped up and shaped into present constitutional rules by the Court. Its decisions about enforcement priorities reflect a choice about which of our pasts is recapitulated into our present and flung forward into the future.

By history and logic, structural constitutionalism appeals to constituencies quite different from those who benefit from individual rights. By and large, the project of shielding the individual from the coercive power of the state was first taken on seriously in the Reconstruction period following the Civil War. Of course, the 1791 Bill of Rights had early on constrained the federal government, but there was simply not all that much to be constrained until the 1880s because of the thinness of the national state. It was instead the 1867 habeas statute and the 1871 Ku Klux Klan Act that became keystones for remedies against state violence. The federal courts took those statutes seriously as remedies for vulnerable minorities only when the structural violence of Jim Crow became a partisan and geostrategic liability. That shift in judicial priorities, while it lasted, benefited groups long relegated to the peripheries of the American story, thanks to their race or ethnicity. In particular, Black men and women like Lula Brawner and Clyde Brown have long experienced the despotic state in its most raw form. More recently, it has also been those like Sergio Adrián Hernández Güereca, along with the victims of the Japanese American internment, the Lavender Scare, and the Travel Ban, who have most acutely felt the force of growing federal power. The withdrawal of judicial remedies for state violence, therefore, most profoundly affects the already marginalized in American society.

In contrast, contemporary doctrines of federalism and the separation of powers both take historical and ideological cues from the Founding period. To the extent that federalism and the separation of powers are concerned with the constraint of state power, therefore, they limit the despotic state in quite different ways, and to quite different ends, from individual negative rights. Their political economy differs starkly. Structural principles offer an etiquette for the exercise of government power, not necessarily a flat limit on its reach. They do not operate with great strength when the state is immediately engaged in coercion. So they typically impose no friction on the harms inflicted by the state upon marginalized and subordinated groups. To the contrary, structural principles recognized by the Court tend to bite hardest when the state is regulating with the aim of *preventing* harms to vulnerable populations. So they are likely to be of greatest use to those who are regulated by the state insofar as they are already inflicting harms to others. Perhaps a version of federalism or the separation of powers that favors the vulnerable and the marginalized can be imagined. But it is not our law.

Judges' taste for enforcing structure over rights today reflects a preference for the political economy of 1789 over the dispensation of 1865. The structure of the Constitution of 1787 accommodated slavery and white supremacy. It did this not just through the infamous Three-Fifths Clause—which gave slave states a boost in population-based representation in the House—but also through the basic structure of the federal government. In particular, the forms of the Senate and Electoral College reflected the slavocracy's influence. The pivotal vote during the Philadelphia Convention favoring the Great Compromise—the keystone of our present bicameral, federalism-infused structure of national representation—was cast by North Carolina on the basis of its interest in slavery.[17] That the structural constitution should be wielded today by lawyers and investment "advisors" eager to prey on the financially weak, hoping desperately for "Buckets of Money," should therefore come as no surprise. The elevation of this element of the Constitution reflects a decision to prioritize the kind of interests that dominated the early Republic over the kind of interests that came to the fore in the Civil War's aftermath.

The Justices' allocation of remedies between individual rights on the one hand and structural ideals on the other is an act of fidelity then to a certain strand of history, and a derogation of another. As such, it is a moral choice. History contains entangled multitudes, struggling against each other for voice or hegemony. The Court's election among various histories, cloaked in the reverent rhetoric of Framer worship, works a benediction on racialized hegemony, while manifesting a malign neglect for the past and present voices of those marginalized, brutalized, and murdered by state violence.

REMEDIES AND THE FUTURE OF THE AMERICAN STATE

The decision to prioritize the Constitution of 1789 over that of 1865 flows from the shifting commitments of partisan coalitions responsible for appointments and jurisdictional choices during the 1970s and the 1980s. It carries those commitments forward in time. The dogged pursuit of superficially neutral structural constitutional principles extends and entrenches a deregulatory agenda that came to dominate both parties' agendas from the late 1970s.[18] Structural constitutional litigation is a way to limit the absolute scope of the federal regulatory state on federalism grounds. It is also a means of durably calcifying the institutional channels through which regulation emerges. The appointment-and-removal-related lines of cases that Seila Law, Beckwirth & Watts, and Raymond Lucia pursued all have a short-term effect of creating uncertainty and delay in the regulatory process. In the long term, they increase the power of the White House, while undermining the autonomy of the federal civil service. Although this might make regulation easier, say when a Democrat is in the White House, its main effect is likely to render regulatory continuity more difficult to sustain.

A political coalition wishing to address a serious national policy problem—whether environmental, public health, or immigration-related—has to grapple with the probability that it will be delayed or derailed by a structural constitutional challenge in the courts. Increased uncertainty, and the inability to durably insulate policy projects, undermines efforts to address long-term national challenges such as climate change or the pervasive weakness of America's public health infrastructure. In this way, federal courts' solicitude for the despotic state, coupled with their unerring scrutiny of the regulatory state, bend the arc of future state development. The denial of remedies to Alexander Baxter, Sergio Hernández, and Amy Hughes makes it easier and cheaper—in dollars and reputation—to deploy the coercive armatures of the state. The judiciary has thus created a constitutional milieu in which there is every reason to avoid legislating new rules as a means of solving social problems—and every reason to double down on the bare use of violence.

No doubt the Court was not the only or the most important political actor in these events. But the Court's remedial interventions have still abetted corrosive and unraveling dynamics that have characterized early-twenty-first-century America. It is difficult to perceive ways in which they have knitted together the social fabric where it has been fraying. And it is well-nigh impossible to avoid the fact that these decisions have ultimately left the nation more fragile, less equal, and more tumultuous.

Coda

You are statistical, You are worked around, You have no recourse. . . . You are easily jailed and easily forgotten. The stakes are low, And so: contempt.
Zadie Smith[1]

WHAT, THEN, DOES an independent judiciary do? For whom does it work? For many people, the idea of independent courts brings to mind hope—the aspiration toward an institution that stands apart from, and brings to heel, the great powers of society. In a democracy under a written constitution, courts are likely to be associated with the hope of keeping officials within the bounds of their lawful authority. So it is in America. But this understanding of what courts do traces its lineage back to an idea most famously offered by Albert Venn Dicey, a professor of English law at Oxford during the Victorian era. For Dicey, the rule of law existed when no person could be made to "suffer in body or goods except for a distinct breach of law established in the ordinary legal manner before the ordinary Courts of the land." In Dicey's vision, any subject of the Queen whose rights were violated by an official ought to have recourse to "the ordinary Courts of the land," where judges steeped in England's ancient common law would vindicate all their rightful claims.[2] These ordinary courts, for Dicey, stood between the state and the people. And, crucially, they were open to all, regardless of rank or station, color or creed.

It would go too far to say that federal courts have never played this role. In the early Republic, federal courts did occasionally use the procedural impedimenta of the common law as a means for keeping state, and sometimes federal, officials under the leash of law. Largely relying upon the Contracts Clause, however, this early strain of constitutional remediation mostly benefited the moneyed. Fugitive slaves received less solicitude. During Second Reconstruction, judges briefly aligned with a racially progressive national faction within the Democratic Party. The combination of geopolitical and intraparty compulsions elicited, however briefly, a judiciary committed to rolling back Jim Crow. Federal judges scoured the statute books for tools to further that end. They found instruments that had until then lain in desuetude. These, supplemented with remedial innovations, were fielded to help those at the sharp end of state violence. In so doing, the federal courts aligned themselves (again, all too fleetingly) with the larger goal of a transformative egalitarian order rather than preservation of an antebellum-rooted White supremacist order.

Paradoxically, federal judges took this stand against the backdrop of a steady secular increase in "despotic" state power at both the state and federal level. How did they not disrupt this trend? The story for the national government is straightforward. Aside from *Bivens*, few federal actions were invalidated during this period. Judicial interventions respecting criminal justice and education also increased effectual federal power to the detriment of subnational bodies. What, though, of the states? Perhaps by smoothing the rough edges of state violence, the courts helped to soothe public concern about their growing police apparatus. Perhaps, contrary to Richard Nixon's fulminations, judicially imposed legality greased the rails for the subsequent exorbitant growth of the carceral state, which (to emphasize) was largely a product of local and state action. Yet at the same time, the federal courts, imperfectly and haphazardly, occasionally gave voice and legal agency to those otherwise rendered mute and marginalized by the growth of coercive state power. To disregard these rare cases in which plaintiffs have prevailed because they did not cut the prison state completely down to size is to miss their best moral and practical justification.

Yet the underlying dynamics that enabled federal courts to play this midcentury role would subsequently undermine their incentives to do so. Changes to the dominant national political coalition that exercised hegemony in the 1970s, as worries about crime soared and political commitments to racial transformation waned, have exerted a constraining gravitational tug on the scope of individual remedies now for a half-century. The justifications for remedial retreat have sounded primarily in worries that officials will be chilled in the diligent pursuit of their duties. But this reasoning is belied by the pervasiveness of liability insurance from the days of the *Flying Fish* case onward. It is also undermined by the sheer size of the coercive American state, which daily gives the lie to the idea that it is an efficient one with no excess needing trimming. The coercive state has been unleashed without any good practical justification.

Worse, having abandoned the role Dicey conjured when it comes to the despotic state, the Court has installed itself as guardian of the structural constitution. This has been to the great benefit of firms trying to avoid regulatory mandates, which are often imposed with the goal of preventing spillover harms. The net effect of this structural turn has been that the public good of constitutional adjudication has been reallocated from the weak and marginalized toward the powerful and harmful.

This inconstant role of the federal courts results from its incomplete separation from politics. It is democratic, but not consistently or always usefully so. The Constitution's framers left the courts open to transient partisan pressures through their structure and appointment mechanism. Founding foresight also failed by overestimating the worth of an individual-center conception of judicial independence. And the Framers failed to consider what goals judges would pursue, if indeed they achieved a measure of institutional autonomy. As a result, the imagined aspiration of judicial independence many find in the document's text stands at some distance from its actual, unanticipated operation on the ground. These structural weaknesses cannot be easily fixed, moreover, because they are hardwired into clear constitutional text. The Constitution is well-nigh impossible to alter formally because of the supermajority voting rules for amendments in Article V. So long as this element of the Constitution remains the law, therefore, we are stuck with Hamilton's failed presuppositions.

That does not mean, though, that nothing can change. A first step would be to remove the blinders that have obscured our understanding of the Court's effect on American society. Popular and elite attitudes in respect to the Court are fixed in postures of abject supplication or blind deference. Too many members of the public accept uncritically the Justices' self-serving claims to stand beyond politics, even though this is quite implausible given the porous infrastructure of Article III. Too many think of the Court principally in terms of its role in school desegregation, and pay culpably little heed to the highly regressive ways in which the Court has protected and enabled the despotic state more recently. Federal courts, as good *federales*, too often refrain from any supervisory role when it comes to state coercion.

The judiciary, moreover, has husbanded not just its former reputation as a foe of Jim Crow, even as it does more to defend wealthy White parents' interest in monoracial schools, but also its allies in the bar and the law schools well. Too many lawyers and scholars genuflect before the federal courts because their own professional standing is inextricably linked to the judges for whom they worked and the federal cases they have filed. They offer simpering local disagreements in an effort to seem relevant. Yet they rarely pause to consider the structural reasons for the judiciary's regressive and decidedly nonneutral role in American state-building. They lean on the lazy, tired, and false assumption that the Court of course plays a binding and healing role, knitting together the disparate and contrary parts of a polity otherwise rent by race, ethnicity, wealth, and status.

Instead of thinking about federal courts as primarily bastions of the rule of law, therefore, we should start to see them as what they are: instruments for the redistribution of the valuable quasi-public goods of constitutionality and legality. The federal judiciary has certainly produced those goods in the course of implementing policy agendas blocked in the elected branches. This has been the case from the beginning of the nineteenth century, when Federalists and Jeffersonians tussled over the size and function of the federal courts, creating and destroying tribunals in a grim tit-for-tat. It continued in the 1870s, when the courts became an instrument for the nationalization of the economy to the benefit of large new corporations and businesses, and again in the 1940s, as a new partisan coalition focused on racial egalitarianism for a complex tangle of partisan and geopolitical reasons. The remedial recession of the past fifty years is just another turn of the knife. This time, judges are moving the law in a direction that enabled a larger coercive state and ensures a weaker regulatory apparatus. Legality and compliance with federal law are, as a result, becoming increasingly unevenly distributed goods under our Constitution. Not everyone benefits, even if these judicial shifts are in an important sense linked to changes in the ruling coalition's composition. When you are picked out by a directly coercive agency, you are more at risk of violent harm. When you are a person or a business subject to federal regulations, you have a larger arsenal of defensive arguments at your beck and call.

Could we do better? A central normative lesson from the history told here is that judicial power, as the object of political construction, has always been the object of legislative action. In that sense, contemporary judicial power is thoroughly democratic in origin; complaints about its nondemocratic quality misunderstand the federal courts' structure and history. In the 1860s and the 1940s, elected actors found ways to recalibrate jurisdiction and to staff the bench to allow, however momentarily, a meaningful provision of legality to subordinated populations. In both moments, judicial action played an important role in creating conditions in which those communities could exercise a degree of real political agency. The judicial vindication of negative rights, in other words, has historically been correlated with an enlargement of democratic participation on the part of subaltern groups.

If the rule of law is built through democratic politics, it is mainly through democratic politics that it can be undermined. Because there are national ruling coalitions that resist the rule of law, and that are content to see the sphere of democratic participation narrowed, the courts have played a regressive role for a half-century. Perhaps a new political coalition will form one day, and commit anew to Albert Dicey's vision of the rule of law as a real constraint on state officials. A coalition concerned with a more equitable and less racially hierarchal society would surely have such a goal in mind. It would, though, have to overcome the structural biases of the Senate and the Electoral College. That coalition could enact new statutes that press the courts into more deliberate service in favor of inclusion, dignity, and popular voice. This would require (at the very least) dismantling the fault limitation on constitutional remedies, ensuring the general availability of *Bivens* rights of action even in immigration and national security contexts, and establishing new evidentiary frameworks that enable private litigants to surface and context discriminatory and irrational state behavior. Such new legislation would also have to ensure that courts are constrained from creating new exceptions to remedies, or from watering down substantive rights as a way of lowering their workload. All this would start to abate the backsliding from the Second Reconstruction era, and the looming desuetude of Section 1983 and the 1867 habeas statute. But all this likely requires not just new jurisdictional and substantive statutes. It also needs new judges.

Such an enacting coalition should be able to seek to channel judicial power back toward the goal of checking illegal state coercion, while also reining in its power to serve as a free-ranging innovator of constitutional theories to use against the regulatory state. The scope of Congress's power over jurisdiction is such that it is possible, even easy, to simultaneously mandate individual remedies while also fencing in the Supreme Court's power to serve as a free-ranging censor of national public policy. The sheer extent of the elected branches' control over federal court jurisdiction is not just a problem. It is also an opportunity. Just because that democratic power has been misused in the past does not mean it cannot henceforth be a motor for institutional improvement. The positive good that federal courts can offer against random and systemic state violence alike can be harnessed, but only if the opportunity is discerned and grasped.

Like many young lawyers, I was inculcated into the law with the haloed imagining of the hero judge, revered for standing up to the lawless state, seared onto my retinas. As it happened, I was also lucky enough to work for two people who fit that ideal, both paragons of decency and righteousness. But with noble and important exceptions, this is not the federal bench we have. Mistaking the actual operation of the federal courts for an ethereal vision of what might have been, and what we might want to do, does nothing to clarify or improve the present deficit of remedies against the coercive state. Until then, the aura of judicial independence should not be confused with the actuality of courts as abettors of a needlessly cruel and despotic state. Until then, we must take courts for what they are and not what we hope them to be.

Notes

...

INTRODUCTION

1. On May 22, 2012, Justice Scalia visited the University of Chicago, and lectured in my Constitutional Law class. This was his answer, or at least my recollection of it, to a student's question of why the Court didn't enforce federalism limits on the national government more rigorously.

2. Seila Law LLC v. Consumer Financial Protection Bureau, 140 S. Ct. 2183 (2020).

3. Petition for Certiorari in *Baxter v. Bracey*, April 8, 2019, https://www.aclu.org/sites/default/files/field_document/baxter_petition_for_certiorari.pdf.

4. Jonathan Sumption, *Trials of the State: Law and the Decline of Politics* (London: Profile Books, 2019), 6–7.

5. Quinn Slobodian, *Globalists: The End of Empire and the Birth of Neoliberalism* (Cambridge, MA: Harvard University Press, 2018), 7

6. Marbury v. Madison, 5 U.S. 137, 166 (1803).

7. Dan Ernst, *Tocqueville's Nightmare: The Administrative State Emerges in America* (New York: Oxford University Press, 2014), 44.

8. Adam Liptak, "Chief Justice Defends Judicial Independence after Trump Attacks 'Obama Judge,'" *New York Times*, November 21, 2018.

9. Joseph Raz, "The Law's Own Virtue," *Oxford Journal of Legal Studies* 39.1 (2019): 1.

10. Albert Venn Dicey, *Introduction to the Study of the Law of the Constitution*, 8th ed. (1885; London: Macmillan, 1902), 182–83.

CHAPTER 1

1. "And yet it moves." Allegedly, said after Galileo had been forced to recant his arguments for a heliocentric solar system.

2. Alison G. Olson, "Eighteenth-Century Colonial Legislatures and Their Constituents," *Journal of American History* 79.2 (1992): 543.

3. Gordon S. Wood, *The Creation of the American Republic: 1776–1787* (New York: W. W. Norton: 1969), 159.

4. John Locke, *Two Treatises of Government*, ed. C. B. Macpherson (1690; London: Hackett, 1980), 83–84.

5. Jack N. Rakove, "The Original Justifications for Judicial Independence." *Georgetown Law Journal* 95 (2006): 1061, 1064.

6. Wood, 161.

7. Brian T. Fitzpatrick, "The Constitutionality of Federal Jurisdiction-Stripping Legislation and the History of State Judicial Selection and Tenure," *Virginia Law Review* 98 (2012): 839, 858.

8. Farah Peterson, "Interpretation as Statecraft: Chancellor Kent and the Collaborative Era of American Statutory Interpretation," *Maryland Law Review* 77.2 (2018): 712, 715.

9. *Journals of the Continental Congress, 1774–1789, Volume 4* (Washington, DC: Library of Congress, 1906), 230.

10. Ingrid Wuerth, "The Captures Clause," *University of Chicago Law Review* 72 (2009): 1683, 1721.

11. Frederick Schauer, "Amending the Presuppositions of a Constitution," in Sanford Levinson ed., *Responding to Imperfection: The Theory and Practice of Constitutional Amendment* (Princeton, NJ: Princeton University Press, 1995), 147–48.

12. John Ferejohn, "Independent Judges, Dependent Judiciary: Explaining Judicial Independence," *Southern California Law Review* 72 (1998): 353.

13. Max Farrand, *The Framing of the Constitution of the United States* (New Haven, CT: Yale University Press), 79–80.

14. Max Farrand, *The Records of the Federal Convention, Volume 1* (New Haven, CT: Yale University Press, 1996), 104–5

15. Ibid., 125.

16. Ibid., 124–25.

17. Jurisdiction and Removal Act of 1875, ch. 137, § 1, 18 Stat. 470.

18. Henry J. Friendly, "The Historic Basis of Diversity Jurisdiction," *Harvard Law Review* 41.4 (1928): 483–510.

19. Greg Goelzhauser, "Classifying Judicial Selection Institutions," *State Politics and Policy Quarterly* 18.2 (2018): 174–92.

20. James E. Pfander, "Judicial Compensation and the Definition of Judicial Power in the Early Republic," *Michigan Law Review* 107.1 (2008): 5–6.

21. Ibid.

22. Alexander Hamilton, "Federalist 78 and 79," in Clinton Rossiter, *The Federalist Papers* (New York: Signet, 2003).

23. Brutus, "Essay No. XI, N.Y. J., Jan. 31, 1788," in Herbert J. Storing, ed., *The Complete Anti-Federalist, Volume 2* (Chicago: University of Chicago Press, 1981), 417, 419.

24. Ibid., 315–16 ("Letter from the Federal Framer," January 18, 1788).

25. Michael Klarman, *The Framers' Coup: The Making of the United States Constitution* (New York: Oxford University Press, 2016), 349.

26. Farrand, *Records*, 154–55.

27. Ibid., 119.

28. Larry D. Kramer, "Madison's Audience," *Harvard Law Review* 112 (1998): 611.

29. Federalist 78, at 457.

30. Federalist 11.

31. Federalist 78, at 471.

32. Ibid., 467.

33. Jonathan T. Molot, "The Judicial Perspective in the Administrative State: Reconciling Modern Doctrines of Deference with the Judiciary's Structural Role," *Stanford Law Review* 53.1 (2000): 68–81.

34. David P. Currie, *The Constitution in the Supreme Court: The First Hundred Years, 1789–1888* (Chicago: University of Chicago Press, 1992), 3.

35. Federalist 51, at 322.

36. David Fontana and Aziz Z. Huq, "Institutional Loyalties in Constitutional Law," *University of Chicago Law Review* 85.1 (2018): 1.

37. Daryl J. Levinson and Richard H. Pildes, "Separation of Parties, not Powers," *Harvard Law Review* 119.7 (2006): 2311. On this history of the first party system, see Stanley Elkins and Eric McKittrick, *The Age of Federalism* (New York: Oxford University Press, 1995), 195–208.

38. Ryan J. Owens, et al., "Ideology, Qualifications, and Covert Senate Obstruction of Federal Court Nominations," University of Illinois Law Review 2014.2 (2014): 347.

39. Sarah A. Binder and Forrest Maltzman, "Senatorial Delay in Confirming Federal Judges, 1947–1998," *American Journal of Political Science* 46.1 (2002): 190–99.

40. Lee Drutman, *Breaking the Two-Party Doom Loop: The Case for Multiparty Democracy in America* (New York: Oxford University Press, 2020), 2, 24–25.

41. Joshua P. Zoffer and David Singh Grewal, "The Countermajoritarian Difficulty of a Minoritarian Judiciary," *California Law Review Online* 11 (2020): 437.

42. Robert Bocking Stevens, *Law School: Legal Education in America from the 1850s to the 1980s* (Clark, NJ: Lawbook Exchange, 2001), 14–15.

43. Adam Bonica et al., "The Political Ideologies of Law Clerks," *American Law and Economics Review* 19.1 (2017): 96.

44. David Margolick, "At the Bar: A Stalwart Conservative Looks at the Supreme Court and Sees a Majority of Mediocrity," *New York Times*, September 27, 1991.

45. Adam M. Samaha, "Originalism's Expiration Date," *Cardozo Law Review* 30.3 (2008): 1295.

46. Brian Leiter, "Rethinking Legal Realism: Toward a Naturalized Jurisprudence," *Texas Law Review* 76.1 (1997): 267.

47. David Epstein and Sharyn O'Halloran, *Delegating Powers: A Transaction Cost Politics Approach to Policy Making under Separate Powers* (New York: Cambridge University Press, 1999), 47–49.

48. Sean Farhang, "Legislating for Litigation: Delegation, Public Policy, and Democracy," *California Law Review* 106 (2018): 1529.

CHAPTER 2

1. M'Culloch v. Maryland, 17 U.S. (4 Wheat.) 316, 408 (1819).

2. Stuart v. Laird, 5 U.S. (1 Cranch.) 299 (1803), contains the details in the next paragraphs.

3. 2 Stat. 89 (February 13, 1801).

4. Act of Mar. 8, 1802, ch. 8, §§ 1, 3, 2 Stat. 132, 132 (repealed 1911).

5. Alexander Hamilton, "Federalist 78," in Clinton Rossiter, ed., *The Federalist Papers* (New York: Signet, 2003).

6. Jed Glickstein, "After Midnight: The Circuit Judges and the Repeal of the Judiciary Act of 1801," *Yale Journal of Law and Humanities* 24 (2012): 543.

7. 5 U.S. (1 Cranch) 137 (1803).

8. Roger C. Cramton, "Reforming the Supreme Court," *California Law Review* 95 (2007): 1313, 1329.

9. Tara Leigh Grove, "The Origins (and Fragility) of Judicial Independence," *Vanderbilt Law Review* 71:2 (2018): 465, 484.

10. Max M. Edling, *A Revolution in Favor of Government: Origins of the US Constitution and the Making of the American State* (New York: Oxford University Press, 2003).

11. Wythe Holt, "To Establish Justice: Politics, the Judiciary Act of 1789, and the Invention of the Federal Courts," *Duke Law Journal* (1989): 1421.

12. Ibid., 1441-42.

13. Quoted in Gerald Leonard and Saul Cornell, *The Partisan Republic: Democracy, Exclusion, and the Fall of the Founders' Constitution, 1780s–1830s* (New York: Cambridge University Press, 2019), 25–26.

14. Justin Crowe, *Building the Judiciary: Law, Courts, and the Politics of Institutional Development* (Princeton, NJ: Princeton University Press, 2012), 1–2.

15. William H. Rehnquist, "The Changing Role of the Supreme Court," *Florida State University Law Review* 14.1 (1986), 3.

16. Holt, 1517.

17. Alison L. LaCroix, "Federalists, Federalism, and Federal Jurisdiction," *Law and History Review* 30.1 (2012): 205, 207.

18. Richard B. Kielbowicz, "The Press, Post Office, and Flow of News in the Early Republic," *Journal of the Early Republic* 3.3 (1983): 255.

19. Alison L. LaCroix, "The Interbellum Constitution: Federalism in the Long Founding Moment," *Stanford Law Review* 67.2 (2015): 397, 401.

20. Stuart Banner, *How the Indians Lost Their Land: Law and Power on the Frontier* (Cambridge, MA: Harvard University Press, 2005), is a brilliant treatment, esp. Chapters 5 and 6.

21. For a visceral account, see Claudio Santo, *Unworthy Republic: The Dispossession of Native Americans and the Road to Indian Territory* (New York: W. W. Norton, 2020).

22. 2 Stat. 420 (February 24, 1807).

23. 42 Annals of Congress 575 (1824) (Isham Talbot).

24. Crowe, 123–25.

25. Tim Alan Garrison, *The Legal Ideology of Removal: The Southern Judiciary and the Sovereignty of Native American Nations* (Athens: University of Georgia Press, 2002), 5–6.

26. Barron v. Baltimore, 32 U.S. (7 Pet.) 243 (1833).

27. Todd E. Pettys, "State Habeas Relief for Federal Extrajudicial Detainees," *Minnesota Law Review* 92.2 (2007): 265.

28. Griffin v. Wilcox, 21 Ind. 370 (1863).

29. Federalist 17.

30. Stephen Skowronek, *Building a New American State: The Expansion of National Administrative Capacities, 1877–1920* (New York: Cambridge University Press, 1982), 27.

31. James E. Pfander, "Dicey's Nightmare: An Essay on the Rule of Law," *California Law Review* 107 (2019): 737.

32. *Little v. Barreme*, 6 U.S. (2 Cranch.) 170 (1804).

33. James E. Pfander and Jonathan L. Hunt, "Public Wrongs and Private Bills: Indemnification and Government Accountability in the Early Republic," *N.Y.U. Law Review* 85.1 (2010): 1862.

34. Barnitz v. Beverly, 163 U.S. 118, 121 (1896).

35. James W. Ely Jr., "Whatever Happened to the Contract Clause?," *Charleston Law Review* 4 (2010): 371, 376.

36. Ann Woolhandler, "The Common Law Origins of Constitutionally Compelled Remedies," *Yale Law Journal* 107.1 (1997): 77, 99.

37. 59 U.S. (18 How.) 331 (1855); see also Andrew Delbanco, *The War before the War: Fugitive Slaves and the Struggle for America's Soul from the Revolution to the Civil War* (New York: Penguin Books, 2019), 103–6.

38. See, e.g., Iowa-Des Moines National Bank v. Bennett, 284 U.S. 239 (1931); Poindexter v. Greenhow, 114 U.S. 270 (1884).

39. Act of February 12, 1793, ch. 7, 1 Stat. 302 (amended 1850) (repealed 1864).

40. Paul Finkelman, "Legal Ethics and Fugitive Slaves: The Anthony Burns Case, Judge Loring, and Abolitionist Attorneys," *Cardozo Law Review* 17 (1996): 1793, 1798.

41. Jones v. Van Zandt, 16 U.S. (5 How.) 215 (1847); Delbanco, 176–77.

42. Prigg v. Pennsylvania, 41 U.S. (16 Pet.) 539 (1842).

43. Steven Hahn, *A Nation without Borders: The United States and Its World in an Age of Civil Wars, 1830–1910* (New York: Penguin, 2016), 90.

44. Fugitive Slave Act of 1850, ch. 60, 9 Stat. 462 (repealed 1864).

45. James Forman Jr., "Juries and Race in the Nineteenth Century," *Yale Law Journal* 113 (2004): 895, 902.

46. Ableman v. Booth, 62 U.S. (21 How.) 506 (1859).

47. Leonard and Cornell, 105–1143.

48. *Dred Scott v. Sandford*, 60 U.S. (19 How.) 393 (1857); Keith E. Whittington, *Political Foundations of Judicial Supremacy: The Presidency, the Supreme Court, and Constitutional Leadership in US history* (Princeton, NJ: Princeton University Press: 2007), 68–69.

49. Chester W. Wright, *Economic History of the United States* (New York: McGraw-Hill, 1941), 707; Jonathan Rees, *Industrialization and the Transformation of American* Life (Armonk, NY: M. E. Sharpe, 2013), 44.

50. M'Culloch v. Maryland, 17 U.S. (4 Wheat.) 316, 408 (1819).

51. William M. Wiecek, "The Reconstruction of Federal Judicial Power, 1863–1875," *American Journal of Legal History* 13 (1969): 333; Crowe, 148–49.

52. 18 Stat. 470 (March 3, 1875).

53. Philip L. Merkel, "The Origins of an Expanded Federal Court Jurisdiction: Railroad Development and the Ascendancy of the Federal Judiciary," *Business History Review* 58.3 (1984): 336, 337.

54. Crowe, 166–67.

55. Howard Gillman, "How Political Parties Can Use the Courts to Advance Their Agendas: Federal Courts in the United States, 1875-1891," *American Political Science Review* 96:3 (2002): 511, 516–517.

56. Union Pacific Railway Company v. Myers, 115 U.S. 1 (1885).

57. Felix Frankfurter and James McCauley Landis, *The Business of the Supreme Court: A Study in the Federal Judicial System* (New York: Macmillan, 1972), 65–68.

58. Tara Leigh Grove, "The Structural Safeguards of Federal Jurisdiction," *Harvard Law Review* 124:4 (2011): 869–940.

59. 26 Stat. 826 (March 3, 1891).

60. 42 Stat. 837 (September 14, 1922).

61. 43 Stat. 936 (February 13, 1925).

62. Aziz Z. Huq, "The Constitutional Law of Agenda Control," *California Law Review* 104.6 (2016): 1401.

63. Crowe, 199–212.

64. Gregory A. Caldeira, "Public Opinion and the US Supreme Court: FDR's Court-Packing Plan," *American Political Science Review* 81.4 (1987): 1139.

65. William E. Leuchtenburg, "The Origins of Franklin D. Roosevelt's 'Court-Packing' Plan," *Supreme Court Review* 1966 (1966): 347, 359.

CHAPTER 3

1. Bivens v. Six Unknown Named Agents of the Fed. Bureau of Narcotics, 403 U.S. 388, 389 (1971).

2. Brawner v. Irvin, 169 F. 964 (C.C.N.D. Ga. 1909).

3. Hernandez v. Mesa, 140 S. Ct. 735 (2020).

4. Michael Mann, *The Sources of Social Power:* Volume 2: *The Rise of Classes and Nation-States, 1760–1914* (New York: Cambridge University Press, 2012), 59.

5. Lisa McGirr, *The War on Alcohol: Prohibition and the Rise of the American State* (New York: W. W. Norton and Company, 2015), 195.

6. Adam Cox and Cristina M. Rodríguez, *The President and Immigration Law* (New York: Oxford University Press, 2020), 136.

7. Frederick A. O. Schwarz Jr. and Aziz Z. Huq, *Unchecked and Unbalanced: Presidential Power in a Time of Terror* (New York: New Press, 2008), 21–49.

8. James T. Sparrow, *Warfare State: World War II Americans and the Age of Big Government* (New York: Oxford University Press, 2011), 5.

9. J. R. DeShazo and Jody Freeman, "Public Agencies as Lobbyists," *Columbia Law Review* 105.8 (2005): 2217.

10. Philip L. Reichel, "The Misplaced Emphasis on Urbanization in Police Development," *Policing and Society* 3:1 (1992).

11. Sarah A. Seo, *Policing the Open Road: How Cars Transformed American Freedom* (Cambridge, MA: Harvard University Press, 2019), 69–78.

12. Anthony O'Rourke et al. "Disbanding Police Agencies" (draft dated August 2020).

13. Terry v. Ohio, 392 U.S. 1 (1968).

14. Aziz Z. Huq, "The Consequences of Disparate Policing: Evaluating Stop and Frisk as a Modality of Urban Policing," *Minnesota Law Review* 101.7 (2016): 2397.

15. Eric H. Monkkonen, "History of Urban Police," *Crime and Justice* 15.1 (1992): 547, 544.

16. Christopher Muller, "Northward Migration and the Rise of Racial Disparity in American Incarceration, 1880–1950," *American Journal of Sociology* 118.2 (2012): 281.

17. Brian J. Stults and Eric P. Baumer. "Racial Context and Police Force Size: Evaluating the Empirical Validity of the Minority Threat Perspective," *American Journal of Sociology* 113.2 (2007): 507; Soomi Lee, Dongwon Lee, and Thomas E. Borcherding, "Ethnic Diversity and Public Goods Provision: Evidence from US Municipalities and School Districts," *Urban Affairs Review* 52.5 (2016): 685.

18. Ernest J. Weinrib, "Corrective Justice in a Nutshell," *University of Toronto Law Journal* 52.4 (2002): 349.

19. Joseph Raz, *The Authority of Law: Essays on Law and Morality* (New York: Oxford University Press, 2009), 212.

20. Jonah Newman, "Chicago Spent More Than $113 Million on Police Misconduct Lawsuits in 2018," *Chicago Reporter*, March 7, 2019, https://www.chicagoreporter.com/chicago-spent-more-than-113-million-on-police-misconduct-lawsuits-in-2018/.

21. John Rappaport, "How Private Insurers Regulate Public Police," *Harvard Law Review* 130:6 (2016): 1539.

22. Ku Klux Klan Act of April 20, 1871, ch. 22, §1, 17 Stat. 13 (current version at 42 U.S.C. §1983 (2000)).

23. "Limiting the Section 1983 Action in the Wake of *Monroe v. Pape*," *Harvard Law Review* 82 (1969): 1486.

24. Smyth *v.* Ames, 169 U.S. 466 (1898).

25. Habeas Corpus Act of 1867, ch. 28, § 1, 14 Stat. 385, 385–86.

26. Lewis Mayers, "The Habeas Corpus Act of 1867: The Supreme Court as Legal Historian," *University of Chicago Law Review* 33.1 (1965): 31, 38.

27. Ibid.

28. Michael J. Klarman, "The Racial Origins of Modern Criminal Procedure," *Michigan Law Review* 99.1 (2000): 48.

29. Myriam Gilles, "Police, Race and Crime in 1950s Chicago: *Monroe v. Pape* as Legal Noir," in Risa Goluboff and Myriam Gilles, eds., *Civil Rights Stories* (New York: Foundation Press, 2007): 41–61..

30. Monroe v. Pape, 365 U.S. 167 (1961).

31. David Rudovsky, "Running in Place: The Paradox of Expanding Rights and Restricted Remedies," *University of Illinois Law Review* (2005): 1199, 1208.

32. Monell v. N.Y. Department of Social Services, 436 U.S. 658 (1978).

33. Hans v. Louisiana, 134 U.S. 1 (1890).

34. Eric M. Freedman, "*Brown v. Allen*: The Habeas Corpus Revolution That Wasn't," *Alabama Law Review* 51.4 (1999): 1541.

35. "Woe for the Lawyers," *Wall Street Journal*, February 13, 1953, 6.

36. Weeks v. United States, 232 U.S. 383 (1914).

37. Wolf v. Colorado, 338 U.S. 25, 28 (1949)

38. Mapp v. Ohio, 367 U.S. 643, 651 (1961).

39. Carolyn N. Long, Mapp v. Ohio: *Guarding against Unreasonable Searches and Seizures* (Lawrence: University of Kansas Press, 2006).

40. *Bivens*, at 389.

41. Miranda v. Arizona, 384 U.S. 436 (1966).

42. 114 Cong. Rec. 12,936-39 (1968).

43. James E. Pfander and Jacob P. Wentzel, "The Common Law Origins of *Ex parte Young*," *Stanford Law Review* 72.5 (2020): 1269.

44. Matthew D. Lassiter, "The Suburban Origins of 'Color-Blind' Conservatism: Middle-Class Consciousness in the Charlotte Busing Crisis," *Journal of Urban History* 30.4 (2004): 549.

45. Kevin J. McMahon, *Reconsidering Roosevelt on Race: How the Presidency Paved the Road to* Brown (Chicago: University of Chicago Press, 2010).

46. John David Skrentny, "The Effect of the Cold War on African-American Civil Rights: America and the World Audience, 1945–1968," *Theory and Society* 27.2 (1998): 237, 250.

47. Mary L. Dudziak, *"Brown* as a Cold War Case," *Journal of American History* 91.1 (2004): 32, 33.

48. Skrentny at 263.

49. Escobedo v. Illinois, 378 U.S. 478, 489 n.11 (1964).

50. Robert Vargas and Philip McHarris, "Race and State in City Police Spending Growth: 1980 to 2010," *Sociology of Race and Ethnicity* 3.1 (2017): 96, 101.

51. Laura Kalman, *The Strange Career of Legal Liberalism* (New Haven, CT: Yale University Press, 1998), 2.

CHAPTER 4

1. Marbury v. Madison, 5 U.S. (1 Cranch) 137, 166 (1803).

2. Hughes v. Kisela, 862 F.3d 775, 778 (9th Cir. 2016), reversed 138 S. Ct. 1148 (2018).

3. Hernandez v. Mesa, 140 S. Ct. 735 (2020).

4. Supreme Court Rule 10.

5. For example, City of Escondido v. Emmons, 586 U.S. _ (2019); Taylor v. Barkes, 135 S. Ct. 2042 (2015).

6. Pierson v. Ray, 386 U.S. 547 (1967).

7. Wood v. Strickland, 420 U.S. 308, 322 (1975).

8. Harlow v. Fitzgerald, 457 U.S. 800 (1982).

9. Malloy v. Briggs, 475 U.S. 335, 341 (1985).

10. Anderson v. Creighton, 483 U.S. 635 (1987).

11. Hope v. Pelzer, 536 U.S. 730 (2002).

12. Graham v. Connor, 490 U.S. 386, 393 (1989).

13. Daniels v. Williams, 474 U.S. 327 (1986); Parratt v. Taylor, 451 U.S. 527, 543 (1981).

14. 28 U.S.C. § 2254(d)(1).

15. Wright v. West, 505 U.S. 277 (1992).

16. For example, Nevada v. Jackson, 133 S. Ct. 1990 (2013) (per curiam); Metrish v. Lancaster, 133 S. Ct. 1781 (2013).

17. Harrington v. Richter, 562 U.S. 86 (2011).

18. United States v. Leon, 468 U.S. 897 (1984).

19. Illinois v. Gates, 462 U.S. 213, 266–67 (1983) (White, J., concurring).

20. Davis v. United States, 131 S. Ct. 2419 (2011); Herring v. United States, 555 U.S. 135, 140 (2009); Arizona v. Evans, 514 U.S. 1 (1995).

21. Oregon v. Elstad, 470 U.S. 298 (1985); Missouri v. Seibert, 542 U.S. 600 (2000).

22. Hernández v. Mesa, 140 S. Ct. 735 (2020).

23. Ziglar v. Abbasi, 137 S. Ct. 1843 (2017).

24. Ashcroft v. Iqbal, 556 U.S. 662 (2009).

25. Aziz Z. Huq, "Article II and Antidiscrimination Norms," *Michigan Law Review* 118.1 (2019): 47.

26. Ziglar v. Abbasi, 137 S. Ct. 1843, 1861 (2017).

27. Hernández v. Mesa, 140 S. Ct. 735, 744 (2020).

28. 28 U.S.C. § 2679(b)(2)(A).

29. Ex parte Young, 209 U.S. 123 (1908).

30. City of Los Angeles v. Lyons, 461 U.S. 95 (1983).

31. United States v. Armstrong, 517 U.S. 456 (1996); Reno v. Am.-Arab Anti-Discrimination Comm., 525 U.S. 471 (1999).

32. Aziz Z. Huq, "What Is Discriminatory Intent?," *Cornell Law Review* 103.5 (2017): 1211.

33. Butz v. Economou, 438 U.S. 478, 506–07 (1978).

34. John Clegg and Adaner Usmani, "The Economic Origins of Mass Incarceration," *Catalyst* 3.1 (2018).

35. Daniel Richman, "The Past, Present, and Future of Violent Crime Federalism," *Crime and Justice* 34.1 (2006): 377, 399.

36. Adam Cox and Cristina M. Rodríguez, *The President and Immigration Law* (New York: Oxford University Press, 2020), 97–98.

37. David A. Sklansky, "The Persistent Pull of Police Professionalism," in Jennifer M. Brown, ed., *The Future of Policing* (Cambridge, MA: Harvard Kennedy School Program in Criminal Justice Policy and Management, 2011), 344–46.

38. Dean Knox, Will Lowe, and Jonathan Mummolo, "Administrative Records Mask Racially Biased Policing," *American Political Science Review* 114.3 (2020): 619.

39. Eve Brensike Primus, "A Structural Vision of Habeas Corpus," *California Law Review* 98.1 (2010): 1.

40. Peter H. Schuck, *Suing Government: Citizen Remedies for Official Wrongs* (New Haven, CT: Yale University Press, 1983), 81.

41. Joanna C. Schwartz, "Police Indemnification," *NYU Law Review* 89 (2014): 885, 890.

42. Malloy v. Briggs, 475 U.S. 335, 341 (1985).

43. Knox, Lowe, and Mummolo.

44. Vani A. Mathur et al., "Racial Bias in Pain Perception and Response: Experimental Examination of Automatic and Deliberate Processes," *Journal of Pain* 15.5 (2014): 476.

45. Joanna C. Schwartz, "How Governments Pay: Lawsuits, Budgets, and Police Reform," *UCLA Law Review* 63.5 (2016): 1144.

46. Joanna C. Schwartz, "Qualified Immunity's Boldest Lie," *University of Chicago Law Review* (forthcoming 2021).

47. William J. Stuntz, *The Collapse of American Criminal Justice* (Cambridge, MA: Harvard University Press, 2011).

48. Stephen J. Schulhofer, "Criminal Justice, Local Democracy, and Constitutional Rights," *Michigan Law Review* 111.6 (2012): 1045, 1076–78.

49. Clegg and Usmani.

50. Melissa Hickman Barlow, "Race and the Problem of Crime in 'Time' and 'Newsweek' Cover Stories, 1946 to 1995," *Social Justice* 25.2 (72) (1998): 149.

51. Naomi Murakawa, *The First Civil Right: How Liberals Built Prison America* (New York: Oxford University Press, 2014); Vesla M. Weaver, "Frontlash: Race and the Development of Punitive Crime Policy," *Studies in American Political Development* 21.2 (2007): 230

52. Daniel T. Rodgers, *Age of Fracture* (Cambridge, MA: Harvard University Press, 2011), 3, 220.

53. Elizabeth Hinton, *From the War on Poverty to the War on Crime: The Making of Mass Incarceration in America* (Cambridge, MA: Harvard University Press, 2016), 329.

54. Ian Haney López, *Dog Whistle Politics: How Coded Racial Appeals Have Reinvented Racism and Wrecked the Middle Class* (New York: Oxford University Press, 2015), 24.

55. United Steelworkers of Am., AFL-CIO-CLC v. Weber, 443 U.S. 193, 254 (1979) (Rehnquist, J., dissenting).

56. Peter Arenella, "Rethinking the Functions of Criminal Procedure: The Warren and Burger Courts' Competing Ideologies," *Georgetown Law Journal* 72.2 (1983): 185, 247.

57. John W. Dean, *The Rehnquist Choice: The Untold Story of the Nixon Appointment That Redefined the Supreme Court* (New York: Simon and Schuster, 2002), 16.

58. Justin Crowe, *Building the Judiciary: Law, Courts, and the Politics of Institutional Development* (Princeton, NJ: Princeton University Press, 2012), 250–52.

59. William H. Rehnquist, "Seen in a Glass Darkly: The Future of the Federal Courts," *Wisconsin Law Review* (1993): 1, 3.

60. Illinois v. Gates, 462 U.S. 213, 267 (1983) (White, J., concurring).

61. Brosseau v. Haugen, 543 U.S. 194, 201–02 (2004) (Breyer, J., concurring).

62. Harlow v. Fitzgerald, 457 U.S. 800, 814 (1982).

63. Harris v. Reed, 489 U.S. 255, 282 n.6 (1989) (Kennedy, J., dissenting).

64. Hudson v. Michigan, 547 U.S. 586, 595 (2006).

65. Banister v. Davis, 140 S. Ct. 1698, 1711 (2020).

CHAPTER 5

1. Claudia Rankine, *Just Us* (Minneapolis: Graywolf Press, 2020).

2. United States v. Bond, 581 F.3d 128, 132 (3d Cir. 2009), reversed, 564 U.S. 211 (2011); Bond v. United States, 572 U.S. 844 (2014).

3. Knick v. Township of Scott, 139 S. Ct. 2162 (2019); Cedar Point Nursery v. Hassid, -- S Ct. – (2021).

4. Our Lady of Guadalupe School v. Morrissey-Berru, 591 U.S. ___ (2020); Little Sisters of the Poor Saints Peter and Paul Home v. Pennsylvania, 591 U.S. ___ (2020).

5. For example, see James D. Nelson, "Corporate Disestablishment," *Virginia Law Review* 105.3 (2019): 595.

6. United States v. Lopez, 2 F.3d 1342, 1345 (5th Cir. 1993), affirmed, 514 U.S. 549 (1995).

7. United States v. Morrison, 529 U.S. 598, 613 (2000).

8. Nat'l Fed'n of Indep. Bus. v. Sebelius, 567 U.S. 519 (2012).

9. See, e.g., Board of Trustees of University of Ala. v. Garrett, 531 U.S. 356 (2001); Kimel v. Florida Board of Regents, 528 U.S. 62 (2000).

10. Bristol-Myers Squibb v. Superior Court of California, 137 S. Ct. 1773, 1780 (2017).

11. See, e.g., United States v. Danks, No. 98-4147, 1999 WL 33101242 (8th Cir. Aug. 13, 1999) (per curiam).

12. Amanda Hollis-Brusky, "Helping Ideas Have Consequences: Political and Intellectual Investment in the Unitary Executive Theory, 1981–2000," *Denver University Law Review* 89 (2011): 197. On the theory's extensions, see Frederick A. O. Schwarz Jr. and Aziz Z. Huq, *Unchecked and Unbalanced: Presidential Power in a Time of Terror* (New York: New Press, 2008).

13. Free Enterprise Fund v. Public Company Accounting Oversight Board, 561 U.S. 477 (2010).

14. Lucia v. S.E.C., 138 S. Ct. 2044 (2018).

15. City of Los Angeles v. Lyons, 461 U.S. 95 (1983).

16. Aziz Z. Huq, "Removal as a Political Question," *Stanford Law Review* 65.1 (2013): 1.

17. Jeremy C. Pope and Shawn Treier, "Reconsidering the Great Compromise at the Federal Convention of 1787: Deliberation and Agenda Effects on the Senate and Slavery," *American Journal of Political Science* 55.2 (2011): 289–306. On the electoral college, see Paul Finkelman, "The Proslavery Origins of the Electoral College," *Cardozo Law Review* 23 (2001): 1145.

18. Martha Derthick and Paul J. Quirk, *The Politics of Deregulation* (Washington, DC: Brookings Institution Press, 2001), 53–54.

CODA

1. Zadie Smith, *Intimations* (London: Penguin Books, 2020), 63.

2. Albert Venn Dicey, *Introduction to the Study of the Law of the Constitution*, 8th ed. (1885; London: Macmillan, 1902), 182–83.

Index

. . .